MARY OF THE *Shanty*

A NOVEL BY

MARY SEATON

Paperback: 978-1-960861-39-9
eBook: 978-1-960861-40-5
Library of Congress Control Number: 2023910828

This is a work of fiction.

SWEETSPIRE LITERATURE
——— MANAGEMENT ———

Chapter 1

*I*t was a cold afternoon in July of 1918, on the bank of the Murrumbidgee River and Jim was having no luck catching a gold perch for his dinner. A Murray cod would also be very nice he thought as he pulled his line out and stared dismally at the piece of wood on the end of it. Jim thought, just as dismally, about the can of bully beef he'd have to make do with for dinner. 'Oh well' he told himself just as cheerfully as he could, 'I should think myself lucky I have a tin of bully beef.'

Jim rolled his hand line up and got slowly to his feet, he was feeling the winters a little more lately. He wasn't sure how old he was, but he thought probably about forty-eight. He'd never been the same since the tractor rolled over on him back in 1897.

Putting his fishing gear in the hut he went to his vegetable patch and got two carrots and a swede to go with the tin of beef. He had potatoes from last season, but he used those sparingly, it would be at least a month before any more were ready. He'd use bread instead, Jim traded for his loaf of bread each month. When that ran out it was damper.

Back in the hut he lay his weary bones down on the bed to rest a while. He'd bought 100 acres on the bank of the Murrumbidgee just outside of town. He'd sold the forty acres his father had bought just out of Granya in Victoria when he'd arrived here from Scotland in 1849. There were just too many bad memories on the place for Jim.

His father had been a violent drunk and had abused him and his mother almost weekly until he was fourteen when he'd stood up and bashed him back. His father didn't throw him out because he could never remember who'd given him the hiding and assumed it was just a pub brawl or something. He'd died when he fell from his horse on his way home from town, stone cold sober and had hit his head on a rock. Loss of blood and the freezing night had done the rest and that was the verdict.

Jim was close to his mother, and he looked after her as best he could. But his mother died soon after a broken woman. Jim buried her alongside his father and put the place up for sale that same day.

'Why didn't you leave the bastard mum' he'd whispered as the tears slid down his cheeks. He'd stood there staring at his mother's grave for ages, he knew why. It all seemed so long ago he mused now, and he still wasn't clear as to whether or not he should have buried his mother the hell away from his drunken mongrel of a father. He shrugged now.

Jim seldom went into Balranald, preferring to stay away from the place with all its people. He went in once a month to sell his milk and cream and eggs. He also sold fruit and veg on these trips. On the first Wednesday of every month, he'd load up his cart with produce and take it the mile or so into town. He had a horse, but he seldom felt like pulling a cart. Occasionally Jim pulled a smaller cart himself.

Afterwards he'd go to the shops for a few things he couldn't grow, shoot, or raise and then he'd call in at the pub where he had two beers and got his drink to take home. He sometimes bought a bag of wheat for his chickens, but he almost always had this dropped off by cart from the farmer out along the road to Gundagai.

Jim opened his eyes and looked about; it was getting dark. 'Shit' he said to himself, 'I must have bloody dozed off.' He got off the bed and lit his tilly light. After he'd had his tea, he drank the last of his flagon of wine. He drank a flagon a month and used the empty and others he'd collected over the years for milk. Jim always wondered if the people who bought up all his milk liked it because it had a wine flavour to it. But buy it they did, and Jim always made enough money to get by and sometimes he put a bit by besides. He had a nice little

2

nest egg which he'd added to his inheritance hidden away.

The next morning the sky was heavy with clouds and Jim got out early to fish. It was a peaceful morning with only the warbling of the magpies and the odd cries from the white cockies to break the silence. He settled himself down with some water and a sandwich he'd made with the left-over bully beef.

He needed to get a supply of fish to smoke. He sat for an hour before he got his first bight, after that he caught them, pretty much, one right after another until he had twenty fish. He decided that would do, that would give him ten to take to market and ten for himself. For some reason people bought up every fish he took to market. He always used blue gum for the smoke but maybe the proof was in the brine he soaked them in beforehand.

Jim had scaled and gutted the fish and was threading them onto a stick to take up to the hut when he spotted a tribe of people coming up the river. They hailed him and stopped to talk amongst themselves for a while. Jim watched and waited; he always spoke some to these people when they came by.

But today they were different, Jim sensed there was trouble of some sort in the group. The voices got louder and more aggressive and he noticed that they seemed to be picking on a young woman with light coloured skin. He watched, not wanting to interfere. The woman they were picking on looked to be a white woman and the argument was getting very heated.

Suddenly one of the other women, an older woman ran up behind her and hit her over the head with a lump of wood. The young woman collapsed, and Jim had seen enough. He ran down the riverbank towards them, yelling for them to stop. They were all hitting her now though she hadn't moved since she'd hit the ground.

One of the older men gave a shout and the whole tribe disappeared into the bush. Jim walked down to the woman on the ground and knelt down beside her. She was breathing but some of the gashes were quite deep. He lifted her head and saw there was blood coming from a wound there at the back of her head.

Jim, a big strong man, had at one time been a fireman and he lifted her onto his shoulder without much trouble. He got her back to his hut and lay her down on a mat on the floor in front of the wood stove where it was warm.

Jim's hut was a two-room affair with good wood at the walls and floor. One room was his kitchen living room and the other his bedroom.

He gazed down at her; she was white as far as he could tell but what was she doing with a tribe of aboriginals. Then Jim noticed that her nose was broad, and her eyes were big. Other than that, he thought she…. Jim was nonplussed, he'd just have to wait till she wakened.

She woke up with a start after about a half an hour had passed and tried to sit up. Her eyes were deep liquid brown and full of fear. Jim put a restraining hand on her shoulder and said, 'don't be afraid. You were hurt so I brought you here, you'll be safe here. Lay still while I get these gashes to stop bleeding.' She remained silent while Jim dressed her wounds.

The strange woman lay still as she was told and gazed steadily back at him. He finished cleaning her cuts and smiled at her. When she smiled Jim thought his heart skipped a beat. It was beautiful, she was beautiful. He smiled back at her. Jim went about sticking band aides all over her.

When he finished, he stood up and said, 'would you like a cuppa?'

She studied him now and Jim thought she probably didn't speak any English; well, he didn't even know what she spoke let alone if he'd understand it. But then in English that was every bit as good as his own she said, 'yes please, that'd be lovely.'

Jim smiled and put the kettle in the centre of the stove again. In a few minutes he poured two cups of tea and handed one to his visitor. 'What's your name' he asked politely?

'Lilly' she said and grinned. She had beautiful teeth. 'Lilly, what a lovely name.'

He watched her as she drank her tea, 'why did they hit you' He asked?

She dropped her eyes and looked at the floor. He was about to apologise when she looked up at him. 'Because I wouldn't obey their laws.'

'Wow, I thought they were going to kill you. They may well have if I hadn't chased them off.'

'Thanks.'

'Oh no need to thank me.' Jim thought for a bit and went on hesitantly. 'What law could have been so important as that?'

'I had been betrothed to an old man who I didn't love. I refused to have anything to do with him.' She blushed and looked away.

'Well alright. Do you have any other family you could go to?'

'No, I have no family, that's why I was with them. I am very distantly related to some of them.'

'Well, you can stay here till you are well enough I've got fish I must see to.

Lay there for a while hay? And then I'll come in and get us some dinner.' He smiled now, 'probably fish.'

It had been two weeks since Lilly had come to stay, and Jim liked having her around. Some of the urges he was getting he thought would one day spoil thing but......

He had given up his bed for her and was busy making another one, this one he'd put in the kitchen by the table and sleep in it himself. Jim got a second- hand mattress in town and brought it home in the cart.

Lilly had caught on tending to vegetables and looked after the fruit trees as well. She fed the chickens how he'd told her and every afternoon she collected the eggs.

Then came the first Wednesday of the month and he took her with him into town to the market. Women everywhere talked in whispers and stared openly at her while they did it. Jim was seething inwardly but, like Lilly, he showed nothing outwardly.

When he'd sold all of his wares and did the shopping, he bought a bit extra. He'd had to set rabbit traps this last week to feed them both. Jim took what was left from his pocket and decided he'd forego his flagon and take Lilly for lunch. As he sat across from her watching the delight on her face as she tackled a nut sundae he smiled. With a jolt Jim realised he liked this woman and wanted her to stay.

When she was finished, he got to his feet and left the café, how was he going to hide how he felt? As soon as he got home, he found things to do outside. At sundown he was at a loss what to do. Maybe he should have got the flagon, he could have drunk it and slept, senseless under a tree.

When Jim walked in the back door, he noticed Lilly looking at him strangely.

'Sorry Lilly, just a few things to '

'Yes Jim' she broke in, 'I know I saw you. I saw you looking for things to do outside. I'm sorry I make you feel so awkward in your own home Jim that you feel the need to do that. I will leave in the morning Jim if that's alright.' She put the tea towel down and came towards him. 'I want to thank you for being so very good to me Jim.'

'No Lilly, oh no that's not how it is. I was looking for things to do outside because I have an almost uncontrollable urge to take you in my arms. I want to hold you Lilly, but I am older and not good looking' and Jim stopped talking as Lilly walked right up to him, 'Me to' she murmured, 'oh Jim…. me to.'

As Jim's arms went round her, he knew he loved her. 'I love you Lilly, I love you very much. I never want you to leave but having said that I won't try to stop you if you need to.' He stopped talking as her arms went round him and he kissed her. He lifted her up and carried her to the bedroom.

Nine months later Jim came home from the market. Lilly didn't go with him anymore as she was too heavy with child. He walked into the hut, and she was nowhere to be seen. He walked back outside and heard a scream from down near the river.

Jim felt his heart lurch in his chest. He ran to where the noise came from and found Lilly near the water, and he was pretty sure she was having the baby. He knelt beside her as he had done all those months ago and lifted her head into his arms. She smiled up at him, 'oh I'm glad you are home my love.' She was breathing heavily, her face wracked with pain.

'Oh Lilly, what can I do.' He looked around, she had a towel she had bought for the occasion and two rocks. Both rocks were round and smooth, and one was flat on top. When the baby was born, she placed the umbilical cord over the flat rock and struck it with the other. She had severed the cord and sealed the end.

Jim had the baby in his arms and was mesmerised by it. It was a girl, and she was beautiful. She looked like his mother and so he said, 'Lilly we are going to call her Mary. Her name shall be Mary Patricia Smith.'

As the next few days passed the baby flourished but Lilly ailed. She got worse as the days went by and Jim was beside himself with worry. There didn't seem to be anything exactly wrong with her, but she sickened, worse each day. She loved him and he knew it, but she was a little distant. 'We'll go and see the doctor Lilly' he'd said.

But Lilly just shook her head, 'No need Jim, I'm fine.'

It was a Wednesday and Jim came home from town as usual, he'd taken the horse, so he unharnessed it and let it go, making sure it had water. Lilly had seemed a lot better lately, and Jim was relieved. He walked in the house and headed for the bedroom.

The baby, who was six months old now, was crying loudly so he went to the cot. Picking her up he said 'Hush now Mary girl, tell daddy what it's all about hay? Come now, there's a good little bairn.' He laughed as Mary put her hands in his beard and tugged it giggling as she did. How he loved her.

The baby stopped crying and he went to find Lilly. To his horror he found her down in the water floating face down. 'Oh God Lilly' he screamed laying the baby on its back. He ran to the water and dragged Lilly's lifeless body to the bank. He sat and cried, he cried for hours until he was exhausted. The fading light started to dawn on him.

When Jim came to his senses it was to the baby screaming where he'd left it. He crawled to it and picked her up in his arms. How could he live without his Lilly? There seemed to be nothing wrong with her.

He buried her under the tree where she'd given him his daughter. Jim was numb and full of misery.

For the months that followed Jim went through the motions of caring for Mary, but his heart was broken, he was broken. As the month rolled into years he got to the stage where he found joy in the small girl. He was sure she was very beautiful and above average intelligence. How he loved her.

He taught her everything about running the place and even took her to market. He let her miss school to go to market. 'You have to learn this, my girl; this is where all your hard work pays off. If you fail here, then it all fails and it was all for nothing Mary. Now pay attention.'

But Jim was drinking heavily, more and more he left work undone which Mary came home and took care of. Jim had never lifted his hand to his beautiful girl, and she loved him without condition.

He sent Mary to school until she was fourteen. He'd built an extra room of wood and corrugated iron for her. She looked after him and always put him into bed when he was drunk.

Jim never got over his Lilly, the worst part was he never knew what killed her. She could swim like a fish so drowning made no sense. His horse died in the winter of 1936 and Jim followed his old horse in the summer of that same year.

Mary buried her beloved father down by his beloved Lilly. She knew he'd always wanted to go to her but stayed around as long as he could for her. Mary cried for hours when she found his body curled up down by Lilly's grave one arm laying across it.

She wiped her eyes and picked up the shovel. Some of the men came out from town when they heard and brought a preacher to say a few words. Mary cared not for their words nor their presence at his grave, in fact in her mind she offered up a silent apology to her dad.

Some women came to help her arrange a wake. Mary thought they came, made some food, and ate it talked amongst themselves even laughing here and there. And then they had left, leaving Mary with a mess to clean up.

They'd fed themselves at her expense and they had feasted. She'd have been better off if they'd stayed the hell away. Yes, Mary was better off on her own she thought.

Mary cleaned up their mess and cried herself to sleep. She didn't know how she was going to cope.

Mary had heard of the great depression ascending on them. Her father had told her that the economy was collapsing and that many people were homeless and had nothing to eat. There was no work for them, and they would starve. Thousands would die he'd said, 'they'll die in the streets Mary girl. You will need to look to keeping what is yours but don't be blind to the plight of the poor beggars Mary.

To make matters worse we are in a thing which they are calling a dustbowl. Farms have failed all over the world and food is in short supply everywhere now.'

Yes, Mary was best off on her own, she certainly didn't need friends like these people. They came to sticky beak and look down their noses. Mary had chained everything up before they got there.

She'd put locks on everything and hidden much away. They had a secret cache down near the river and that was brimming with vegetables and fruit. There were eggs and milk and some meat. It was basically a hole in the ground lined with wood and things stayed much cooler in there and so kept longer. Mary had helped her father line the hole with boards and put a trap door on it. It was then covered with leaves`.

In the larder she had dried food, jars and tins and bags of flour and sugar. Her father's words came back to her, 'you look after yourself Mary but spare a thought for the poor bastards who come begging. They are probably starving. Keep that bloody gun loaded and get a big bloody dog. You'll need a good horse to Mary' he'd said and that was when he had begun to build a stable right next to the house. 'We can make this window into a doorway and bring the horse in this way. If they want it, they can throw it over the fence hay.' He had laughed and Mary's heart almost broke the memory was so vivid.

He died before he finished it and Mary had never felt more alone and afraid. She snapped out of it, she had to. She'd have to get busy. If her father predicted these events, then Mary had no doubt they would become a reality. She didn't doubt that this was her future and despite the heat of the day she shivered.

She finished cleaning up the mess and looked about her. The house her father had built was strong and secure. Well, she'd make it even more so she thought as she looked in the larder. She didn't know how they'd managed it, but they'd taken off with a good bit of her stuff. Where had they hidden it? What could she expect from starving strangers if her fat friends had treated her like that?

Yes, Mary knew she was better off by herself.

Chapter 2

Mary was almost eighteen and had been alone for eighteen months. She had kept her gardens tended and the chickens fed. Everything flourished in her care. She'd had to dip into her father's nest egg to buy a horse and a dog. She found pulling the cart into town was hard work and took her away from her other farming jobs. So, the horse was a God send. The dog was for protection, it was a blue heeler, blood hound cross and came up to Mary's waist. They didn't come more protective than him.

It was just at the beginning of 1937 and Mary, though she hadn't heard much about it she knew the great depression was upon them and getting worse each year. Government assistance was almost non-existent now.

She kept up with the news on an old radio her father had, and which ran on batteries, so she used it sparingly. The depression was being made worse by what they called the dustbowl which seemed to be running rampant across the world. Mary worried about it all, but she kept on working and growing and adding to her reserves.

She had noticed an influx of very poor and destitute people arriving in town. Some of them had tents which they carried and all manner of goods and chattels. Families came and single men all looking for work, all starving. All carrying everything they owned mostly on their backs. And the children they brought with them were just pitiful and almost never attended school.

They pitched their tents on the outskirts of town or slept under the trees in a big camp. The smells from the camp were unpleasant to say the least. Mary had a rifle but looking at these people, she also purchased a handgun which she always wore in her belt at her side. The Dog she called big Jim was also always at her side.

The council had asked the people in the camps to leave so most of them wound up farther along on the commons on the banks of the Murrumbidgee. They came to rest at the edge of Marys place almost alongside her boundary fence. about a quarter of a mile away from Mary's shanty. She saw what was coming and knew she'd have to brace herself for it, everybody would.

Mary was building a small stable and yard for her horse right next to her hut and opening into her hut via a doorway in her bedroom. The door was only a half door she had thrown together out of offcuts. It didn't keep much of the smell out. Mary would keep her horse close at night and to get Lilly out they'd need to come through the hut and through her bedroom. Lilly and Big Jim had bonded, and Mary was glad. Her dog slept inside on her bed, he also was made of meat, and these were desperate times.

Mary had taken to patrolling the yards two or three times a night at odd times and she took him with her. She wore her gun and carried a rifle. She'd been visited by a couple of hobos whom she'd fed and given them food and water. She gave them some old jackets of her fathers which were much better than the ones they had on.

Her horse was called Lilly of the Valley, she just called her Lilly and Mary lead her into her stable through the hut before dark every day. Lilly seemed to like it and never objected, of course the bit of hay Mary gave her helped.

When the stable was done, she began making her hut more secure. She had put the bulk of her money in a hole in a tree that the cockies nested in every year. When she put her money in it, she placed a piece of bark over the opening to keep the weather and animals out as well as hiding her money. The rest of the money she'd put in the wheat in the chickens feed drum which she kept in the lean to.

On this occasion Mary was building a chicken coop Right next to the hut so she could see them from her window. She had three dozen chickens and a rooster. They had a dozen baby chickens about half grown and Mary knew she had too many. But she couldn't bring herself to get rid of them. And she almost always sold all her eggs.

Mary chopped the head off the rooster and ate him so he wouldn't attract attention to her chickens with his crowing. It was a bit drastic she knew but she needed some meat anyway.

At night Mary herded these chickens into the coop at the side of the hut and used a padlock on their door. She'd built it high enough to have a roost, Mary had had to put three roosts in to accommodate them all. They soon got used to the new routine and went in there themselves.

Her goats and cows were a bit easier she tethered them at the door under the lean-to veranda at night. In the daytime she had to let them go and graze, so she had to leave what she was doing often to go look at them. Where she had them tethered, she put bells on their rope so if there was a struggle, she'd hear it.

There was a shed next to the house which Jim had built, and he had built it very strong and had put a door on it. Mary had bought a padlock at the market and locked the shed up with it. She had such a lot in that shed that she didn't want stollen. There were boxes and boxes of things she'd bought from the travelling hawkers. Mostly offcuts of materials and building materials. There were tools, drums, and bags. Mary had all of her seeds stored in the shed, seeds for gardening and a bag for wheat, good wheat for planting. She had it firmly in mind that one day she would farm this place.

Mary was ever alert and found she hated market days. She had put a door on a lean to veranda on the back of the shanty which her father had built. She put the two cows and three goats in there while she was away. The two nanny goats had babies numbering four in all. It was a bit crowded and took some mucking out when she got home.

Mary was grateful that her father had never built anything that wasn't strong enough to withstand hail, gale, male and female. He had taught her to do the same. Their buildings weren't flash by any means, but they were strong.

Mary was on her way home from the markets when she saw her most disturbing of visions. It was a few feet from her fence line and three children were playing in the dirt. She never knew children could be so skinny and still be alive. When they stood up to wave at her she marvelled that they could and that their legs didn't break. Their shirts were torn, and their ribs were visible through the skin.

She stopped her horse and asked them if they'd like a ride. They were up on the horse squealing their delight within moments. After she told them her name she said, 'why don't you show me where you live, I'd like to meet your mother.'

One of the boys directed Mary to their mother's tent, and she got down and got the children down. Pulling her jacket, one of her father's old jackets, round her to hide her gun she stood in front of a large but very hungry looking woman. A tall, thin equally hungry looking man stood next to her.

Suddenly Mary was very shy, even humble, but she forced herself to smile back at them. 'Have these little blighters been up to no good Miss', asked the mother fearfully?

'Goodness no' said Mary as she went to her cart. Pulling two flagons of milk from under the tarp she held them out to the woman whose name she told Mary was Iris. She stared at the milk hungrily, 'what Miss?'

'Milk. Please accept it for the children. I will bring you a few of these each week.' Mary looked closely at the woman and said, 'I want you to drink a half glass yourself each day.'

'Oh, thank you Miss', Iris started to sniff. 'Thankyou.' She put the flagons on an old table and had to drag her eyes away from them.

Mary had seen some other children about; some were even worse. 'Could you help some of the others out to' asked Mary?

Iris nodded vigorously, 'yes of course Miss. Thankyou. Oh yes all of the children are so hungry here.'

Mary reached back under the tarp saying as she did, 'I don't have much I'm actually quite poor, but you are poorer' she smiled her most dazzling to take the offence out of her words.

She hauled out a bag of potatoes she'd been unable to sell at the market, a twenty-pound hessian bag of potatoes and a ten-pound bag of carrots. Mary also hauled out a two-pound bag of rice which she'd purchased for herself, but she'd make do alright. She lived like royalty compared to these people.

'Oh and wait a minute' she said and handed the husband 2lbs of onions. She turned to them now and said, 'I cannot afford anything more this trip, but I promise you I will do my best to bring something every week. Please cook these up and share the food with everyone.' Mary walked to the front of the cart and handed over a five-pound bag of flour. Most of this she had bought to restock her larder not because she needed them urgently. Mary hadn't grown any onions this time but she still had them hanging at home.

The woman had begun to tremble as tears sprang to her eyes, 'we have very little money, not enough to pay for all this love.'

Mary smiled and waved her hand at the woman 'I'm not looking for payment.'

Iris wiped her eyes and smiled, 'people might have died here my dear. We haven't seen such food in the last few months.'

Mary looked thoughtful and then turned to the husband who also had tears in his eyes. 'Mister....?'

'Roberts Miss, our name is Roberts, I'm Dan.' He told her and shook hands with her. He noticed her strong grip. He noticed also that she dressed in pants and a light blue shirt under her old jacket. He didn't care what she was dressed in she'd just handed them more food than they'd seen at one time in months, maybe even years.

'Well mister Roberts I am willing to turn over a one-acre piece of my land for you to grow food. I will give you seeds and cuttings. You can grow all the vegetables you need on one acre. Are you interested?'

Dan was trying to swallow the lump in his throat and so he nodded his head, 'yes Miss, oh yes. Are you an angel?'

'Well, we'll see. Who knows how long this will go on for? And I will give you some materials to build a chicken coop and give you a dozen chickens, for eggs.' Mary swung up on her horse and remembered she had two big juicy green apples in her saddle bags she'd been too busy to eat.

'Just a minute' she said taking out the apples and handing them down to Iris, 'cut these up and share them out as best you can. Next time I will bring more.' She looked at Dan now, 'I will leave it to you to tell the others. Anyone who wants to work for it fine, but I advise you to inform your people of a no work no eat policy. I will come back tomorrow Mister Roberts and bring seeds and such. I'll be here early and we'll make a start. My land is the other side of that fence over there, we'll start there.' Mary looked thoughtful a moment and said, 'You may want to inform everyone that if anyone steals from me the deal is off and I carry guns and keep my dog for protection at my side.'

Dan smiled and put his hand out which she shook. She went on 'It will take a while to get your own supply going so until then, like I said I will do my best and bring you all that I can. I don't have much to do with people Mr Roberts but that doesn't mean I don't like them, nor would I stand by and watch anyone die of hunger as long as I have food. Unlike some around about.'

Mary looked about then back at Dan 'I work very hard for what I have. If at any time anyone has to venture onto my land, I would like you to be with them.'

She clicked her horse to walk on and turning she waved to the children 'anyone who wants a ride on Lilly tomorrow be at the gate to my land early. Goodbye to you.'

Iris fell into her husband's arms and cried, despite her size Iris was very sick and loose skin hung from her. Mary had noticed and she suspected the woman was beyond help.

Dan sniffed and patting his wife's head he said softly, 'you know Iris? I think we might be okay. God bless that girl.' Yes, God bless her he thought and wondered at her age.

Must be only a kid he thought, probably not much more than eighteen but he knew one thing. He wouldn't be messing with her given the gun she wore under that jacket. And given what she had come to offer, he wouldn't be letting anyone else mess with her, this girl who had come and thrown them a lifeline.

Dan himself was probably ten years older than her and had not a fraction of her nouse. Yes, he nodded he was glad he'd met her. Apart from saving his life he wanted to learn from her, needed to learn from her. He'd got a strange feeling from her, a good feeling. She was strong and confident and beautiful, and he liked that. No, he wouldn't be messing with her, she was their saviour, an answer to his prayers. There was a stirring of excitement in his belly and he liked that to.

Dan called a meeting of all the people in camp and outlined what had happened. Most of the twenty-eight adults there produced tears. There were eight couples and four young women, and the rest were single men. And at Mary's suggestion he told them of his no work no eat policy. Everyone nodded eagerly, they were all bloody hungry and had thought they may die.

They agreed to the no stealing and only going onto Mary's land if accompanied by Dan. They were only too glad to agree, they knew their lives may very well depend on it. This woman called Mary was their saviour and some of them saw the significance of her name and drew a breath.

The men got busy that afternoon with what materials they could get hold of and built a food safe in a tree. It was high up off the ground and they arranged a bit of tin at the trunk to discourage mice and rats, even ants, or certainly make it hard for them. Dan had an old tarp that they would use to cover their food inside the cache.

That night they all ate. A small meal but a meal. The women had cooked some rice and potatoes with a few carrots and an onion. They threw some flour in to thicken it and make it stick to their ribs. Iris had made two dampers to eat with it. Most of them had full bellies and couldn't remember when they felt so good last. The apples were cut up small and shared amongst the children. The milk mostly went to babies with a small drink each for the kids.

———⟶⟶⟵⟵———

Mary had a few misgivings, but she couldn't see them starve and she couldn't keep feeding them all. This way they fed themselves. She decided she'd lend them two rabbit traps to, any more would probably soon mean no rabbits for anyone. She'd also lend them some fishing line and hooks the river was teaming with fish now. She'd throw a dozen smoked fish and six smoked rabbits in the back with another bag of potatoes.

Mary thought she wouldn't make much money at the market this next month, but she had added to the nest egg over the years, so she wasn't short of money. She smiled at how appropriate it was, hiding the nest egg in a cockies nest. Maybe they'd hatch some more, she grinned. And in fact, Mary thought she would not go to the market this month, and sell stuff which those people needed to survive. The money from this week's market would go to flour and sugar and some tea and coffee for the camp.

The other thing was, if they had food, they wouldn't be so inclined to steal from her. Mary wasn't a mother, but she was pretty sure if she had children who were so starving, she would steal for them.

These weren't bad people she mused as she plodded along the track, they were desperate people. Still, she told herself, she'd still be locking away her livestock, at least until they were no longer starving. Hungry was one thing, starving was quite another and now she'd seen it she understood it. Oh, by God she did!

Mary was absolutely certain that her father would have done the same thing. A wind sprang up and rustled the trees and she smiled up at the gum trees he had always so loved. She wondered about Iris she'd have to examine the woman a little closer. From what she had observed, she and her husband Dan had two boys. Mary hated to think that she would die and leave her boys with no mother.

When she got home, she loaded the cart and kept it at the back door. She also tied tins all around the tarp covering it. Mary didn't trust these people yet, maybe she never would. 'Time will tell' she told herself.

She ate some tea and got into bed early, tomorrow would be a big day. She had placed her seeds for planting into a large wooden box with a lid, she had to look after those now.

———∿∿∘♥♥♥∘∿∿———

The next morning Mary was up early before the sun. She took a sugar bag and went out to pick oranges and pears, a bag full. She had some jams left, way too many for her, so she put five jars of it in a box on the cart. Her jams were so delicious and full of fruit you could eat it from a spoon and with it she included a jar of cream. She included a flagon of milk from the cows she'd just milked, and some tea and sugar.

Mary was in the habit of buying half a sheep or several pounds of beef every couple of months, so she put a shank and a flap into a box and up on the cart. There was a nice bit of fat on the flap. She threw in a little dripping as well.

These people needed fat, needed it badly.

She had put the plough on the back of the cart last night and the seeds. Mary wasn't very big, but she was very strong. Even so she used her father's rough made pully to get it up in the back. She also threw two cabbages in a bag for Iris. On inspection of her rough larder Mary discovered she already had two bags of rice. She'd give them one and three pumpkins. She had so many pumpkins go rotten that she was glad to give them away. Lastly, she added a bag of flour to the pile.

She set off with Lilly and this time she had Big Jim with her. He hadn't met these people, so she kept him on a rope. She'd let him snarl at them for a while before she told him to shut up.

She picked up twelve kids at the gate, Mary figured every kid that could walk, she had to get down and lift some of them on. She walked the horse and kept her eye out for kids who were going to topple off though most of the kids sat up in the cart. Big Jim didn't know what to make of them, so she kept him close. She didn't want him getting too friendly just yet.

At the camp Dan and most of the men were waiting for her. She let Big Jim growl for a while to show off his teeth and then she told him to shut up. He sat as he was told and eyed the men carefully as they did him. Dan showed her the makeshift food safe they'd made, and the men all gathered round proud of themselves.

Mary smiled and nodded, 'it is very good' she said convincingly and got smiles from the raggedy bunch of men. But above all she was pleased to see they had tried. And with what they had at hand they had done an amazing job and she told them this to. Their smiles turned into wide grins as they looked as proud as punch.

Jim sat eyeing the kids but sat where she told him. Eventually it got too much, those kids looked to be having a lot of fun. He ran and joined in the frolicking much to the delight of all the kids.

Nodding her head in approval she turned to Dan and said loudly, 'I have some off cuts of this and that you know wood and tin etcetera. I Never throw anything away never know when you're going to need it. I used to go with my father to the tip where he had got most of the materials for our hut. I'll bring these things as soon as we get this planting done. I also brought some chicken wire, just off cuts to make a coop. Use it to house your chickens at night, foxes are bad about.'

Mary went to the cart and took the tarp off; it was an old tarp but a good one. She had decided not to bring her good tarp and had opted for a tarp they could have if they came up with a need and they had. She'd noticed the tarp in the food safe, it was in tatters. She threw it on the ground and told Dan to take it for the good of the community. He snatched the tarp up, his eyes shining bright a big grin on his face. 'Thanks Mary' he said.

The men almost gasped when they saw the plough, they'd thought they'd be digging hard ground for days. Not only that but this mere slip of a girl had loaded it up by herself as far as they knew. Maybe there was a bloke about somewhere.

Iris and two other women came over to say hello and Mary found she was really worried about the woman. She was very sick and Mary knew it. She'd have a look at her later, Mary came from a long line of medicine women and had gone to the local tribe to learn whatever she could. She had also gone to a nurse at the hospital and learned from her.

She handed the three women the fish and rabbits, two cabbages, three pumpkins and the bag of fruit. 'That's all I have that's in season I'm afraid.' She handed Iris a little box with the jars of jam, 'you can eat it from the jar' she explained, 'or put it on damper. Kids will love it and it's good for them. And here's another flagon of milk from the cows this morning.' She handed a woman called Noreen the bag of lamb.

'Oh, you are a Godsend love, we would have lost these blessed little babies, we have two here and one on the way. We decided that if Maisie's baby is a girl, she's calling her Mary.'

Mary smiled at the women. 'Now if you'll excuse me, I need to get these men moving the day is wasting away.'

She handed Dan a large box and said 'there are a couple of rabbit traps and a few old hand lines. The hooks are in the bottom so be careful. The river is teaming with fish. I noticed a few older men who could fish all day and probably be glad to.'

'I know' said Dan smiling, 'we didn't have much luck catching too many fish but now I think we turn the tables on them. Mary, I thank you from the bottom of my heart, you have saved lives here.' He picked up her hand in his, a tear tumbled down his cheek, 'There are no words.' He looked at his wife and Mary noticed the worry lines.

She said softly as she took her hand back, 'do you know what is wrong with Iris?'

Dan shook his head, 'not a clue Mary.' He looked into her eyes, his full of misery. Then he brightened 'but we have work to do. How did you get this thing in the cart girl?'

'A pully.' She spoke quietly, 'I will have a look at your wife Dan, once we get this work done. I know something of illness and natural medicine.'

'Oh, Mary I would be grateful…. So grateful….'

'I know, now let's get out to the paddock' she turned her head to the others 'all aboard' she shouted, and they laughed. As they went passed her most of them thanked her for the meal, they'd had last night. Mary nodded to each and the smile on her face was understanding.

At the paddock the men who knew what they were doing took the reins and started to plough. Mary had sorted the seeds into large tins. She told them, these are carrots, and these are broad beans etc. And they sewed the ground thus. They finished off with cabbages and swedes. A full row of each. Some young men took corn and planted a few rows of that, Mary had instructed them to plant it all round the outside. 'It may offer the garden some protection from the cold winds' she explained.

Two of the men went out with cuttings of pumpkins and put them in the ground. One of the men whose name was Jack commented to Mary at how good the soil was. She watched the young man get down and pick up handfuls and let it run through his fingers. 'My old dad used to say, "if you look after the soil, the soil will look after you." Isn't it so Miss?'

Mary nodded and looked into his very handsome face, 'My father said the very same thing, Jack. If you all look after this soil it will save your lives. If we have a dry spell and we seldom do in this season you can cart water from the river.

But we'll cross that bridge when, and if we come to it.' Mary smiled at him 'your father was a farmer, Jack?'

He nodded and straightened up. 'We grew mostly wheat until too many bad seasons ran him off. He died soon after that and I was made a ward of the state for almost a year. Met up with Dan about two years ago on the road over near Hay. Some of us got jobs with the highways department and it helped out a bit.'

She looked down at his rough hands and realised he'd probably been farming all his life. His voice came to her softly, 'do you know how many lives you have probably saved here Miss. I am very grateful for your kindness and also your wisdom.' He smiled at her and knelt down in the soil. Indicating the ground around him he said 'and this is wisdom Miss, this is very wise indeed, helping us to help ourselves' He plunged his hand into the dark soil, dug into it and planted the cutting and put a pumpkin seed beside it. Picking up another tin he watered it.

In the furrow next to them six men were planting potatoes. They worked hard and Mary was overjoyed at how they shared the work and got it done so quickly and so well. She was glad to notice a few knew what they were doing, and they taught the rest. She was also glad to notice the easy, friendly and open way the interacted with each other and the laughter they shared.

Mary nodded her approval. With this man Jack, and Dan she knew they'd be alright. She said so now, and Jack smiled up at her. Mary gave him a yellow stick to put in the ground which indicated that there were carrots planted here.

Mary had taught Dan how to plough and she watched him now. He was a natural she thought. He looked up and saw her watching and grinned at her, he was pleased with himself and the look on her face.

By teatime that night they had planted enough food to see them through at least a month. They had planted almost a quarter of an acre and had ploughed the rest. They would be out again tomorrow, and they would plant a couple of grape vines as well.

Mary walked over to Dan and said quietly, 'Dan might I suggest that after the next day or so that we stagger the plantings so that you have food to harvest about every month.'

Dan nodded, 'that's a good idea Mary, by the day after tomorrow we will have all these cuttings and these trees. One orange one pear and one apple if I am not mistaken.' Mary smiled and nodded.

'Will you stay and have some tea with us Mary?'

Mary accepted and they left the plough and took the cart back to camp. 'I don't think anyone will run away with it.' She said and they laughed.

Dan was tired but he couldn't remember feeling so good. They had asked Mary to share their meal and Mary stayed. She liked the company, and the food was good. These women had made enough to feed the camp and had made a little food go a long way. Yes, she thought these people would make it and she breathed a sigh of relief. They had thrown the shank and a little fat in with the stew which flavoured it up nicely.

An old man whose name was Samuel sidled up to her and grinned. 'We are going fishing tomorrow me and Ben. Thankyou girl for giving us the means to save ourselves and a little of our self-respect.'

'Oh, I forgot bait.'

Samuel laughed, 'we can manage that, and I will keep a fish for you.'

'How long have you been on the road Samuel?'

'Bout four years. Joined up with Dan and his troupe about two years ago. I'd have been dead if it wasn't for that man there picking me up off the side of the road where I lay. When it rains and its freezing, he lets us sleep in his tent. He is a gift from God himself girl.'

'How many of you don't have tents?'

'Just Maynard me, young Wally, and Ben. Also, a couple of the young blokes. We make do with a bit of tin or whatever we can find. Barring that we huddle together under a bit of tarp. We get a bit of a government hand out which we gladly hand over to the women and they feed us what they can. One day things will return to normal. I hope.'

'Do you like to fish Samuel? '

Samuel nodded and grinned, 'did a lot of it in my youth dear.'

'There are rabbit traps there to, there are a lot of rabbits round about. If you can set traps and fish, you should fair a little better here, the river's teaming with fish just now. I will do what I can Samuel. My dog seems to be enjoying the company of these children, he won't want to come home. I think the tea is dished out Samuel, come let's eat. It smells mighty good, doesn't it? I'm glad I met you all Samuel.'

'It was nothing short of a miracle meeting you, Mary.'

Mary was introduced to everyone and handed a bowl of delicious stew, lamb stew. Everybody ate in silent reverence and Mary was touched. They mostly sat on the ground though some of the older women had drums or stools or just logs of wood to sit on.

Mary noticed that when ever Dan spoke his people listened. He was definitely the leader she thought. And Dan never raised his voice he didn't have to by the looks.

Even the children loved him, some of the younger ones tried to get in his knee. He'd let them for a while and then put them gently down. The young men tried to get him to explain things to them and he was ever patient with them.

He looked at Mary and smiled 'this is a beautiful meal Mary, thank you. I hope our garden grows and thrives Mary and that we can stand on our own feet so to speak.' He looked down and said softly, 'and thank you for teaching me the plough Mary.'

'How do you feel Dan, are you sore' she asked?

Dan laughed softly, 'Oh yes Mary girl, oh yes.' He looked her straight in the eye now, 'I am sore but it feels good.'

Chapter 3

Mary stood at the fence line shaking her head, 'I can't believe it, this acre is being transformed. Where it was all just dark brown dirt is now an oasis of green. From dust bowl to food bowl. All good healthy food for you and your children. You should be proud of yourselves. We were lucky to get that bit of rain though.'

It had been three weeks since Mary had helped these men plant a bit over a quarter of an acre of the paddock. She nodded with staggering the planting, there would be enough food here to feed these people all year. The men were grinning from ear to ear. Mary's face took on a worried look. Everyone stopped talking and sat still, something was up. She turned to face them and sensing something was amiss, Dan spoke. 'What's wrong' he asked softly? Mary could feel that they were all bracing themselves.

Mary started to speak, 'my father always told me if you bring bad news, you'd best bring a solution. Now I do have both, but it will take work…. Lots of it.' She paused and they nodded.

'Go on,' said Jack. He found this girl fascinating. Something happened to his breathing when he looked at her. Something went wild inside him all together that he tried to hide.

Mary went on quietly. 'Well, I went to a council meeting the other night to see if what I had been hearing round about was true. And it seems that they want to push you off the commons. They will find a way, they will. They are mean nasty people most of these people on the council. If it's not there in one of their by-laws, they will just invent one.' Mary stopped speaking but kept her eyes down as she let them digest this piece of news. She looked up and was struck by the despair on their faces. Some faces registered shock and others fear. Some of the women looked at their children and tears sprang to their eyes. So, this was it, they were beaten again.

'Bloody hell, just when we thought things were going smoothly. Just when it looked like we might have a bloody chance hay?' Dans voice shook with emotion. He looked at Mary now and said. 'thank you for your help Mary, Do you have any idea how long it will be?'

Greg spoke, his voice full of his despair, 'well if they are going to have to look for a way, then we probably have a couple of months. Enough to harvest the vegetables and maybe take some with us. But leave we will have to.'

Mary drew a deep breath, 'Now hold on everyone, I have a solution, but it will take hard work like I said. But we can do it.'

'What are you thinking Mary' asked Dan?

'Well, I am prepared to turn another acre or so over to you.' She looked over towards the fence. 'You can take the rest of this patch from the end of the garden right through to the fence line there. There are some nice big trees here. My proposal is that we get busy and build a long hut, like the long houses that the Vikings made.' Mary stopped talking to let it sink in.

Ben the master builder nodded his head, 'we could do it, but it would take some materials.'

'You'd let us?' Dan was speechless, he gaped at the girl.

'Yes, I would. Like I said until somebody disrespects me and my things, we are fine. I will fence these two acres off so that my animals don't eat your garden. See, it works both ways.'

'Mary, I don't know what to say. Thankyou from the bottom of my heart girl.

We owe you so much.'

Mary shook her head, 'Who knows anything about building?'

Dan said 'there's Ben who was a master builder and these two blokes who are builders. A long house Mary…. what an idea.' He looked at the two blokes whose names were Mark and Ron. They nodded eagerly. Dan went on 'we have no building materials and not a lot of tools.'

'Do you have axes or saws?' Mary looked about at them; eight men raised their hands. 'Good we'll start there. If you go along the riverbank, you will find sixteen trees that are marked with a cross. They are not too far away. Cut them down and use them we'll need at least sixteen good strong uprights. They are mostly very tall trees we may be able to use the tops so keep them.'

She looked around at them, 'does anybody know how to build with brush and mud?'

Again, five men raised their hands.

'Good.' said Mary 'tomorrow the men with cutting tools will begin cutting down the marked trees. Who is a tree cutter?' When one man raised his hand Mary said, 'you will supervise that then.'

She drew a deep breath and thought for a moment. 'I know of three houses which have been demolished in the last eighteen months. If one builder and five of the strongest men can come with me, we will go and pick over these cast offs. We'll have to make several trips or hopefully anyway. So today we can start by planning where we will build it and measure it out. If we all pitch in, we may have these children and you all in and out of the weather before the winter hits us, as hit us it will. Does anybody have any ideas, I am not a builder.'

The talk went on and after tea it went on into the night. These people were eager, they were cold, and they were worried about their kids in the winter. It was into March, so they only had weeks or maybe days. Some men were sleeping under lean to's, and the old ones could possibly die.

The next day Mary picked the men up early about seven o'clock. She got there just as Dan was finishing a cup of tea. 'Good morning, Mary' he said with a smile handing his cup to Iris. 'Ben is coming with us to supervise what will be most useful. Will it be alright Mary for some of these young blokes to start shifting the camp over to the garden?'

Mary nodded 'of course, that's a good idea. Get off these blasted commons I say.'

When they got to the dumping site Ben jumped down off the

cart and darted about his eyes darting all over. He was like a big kid. 'Yes, yes', he would say at intervals, and 'Oh very good.' He kept this up for a while then 'Mary I know which pieces are most important. Should we start there?'

'Yes Ben, you know best.'

He grinned at her through his grey beard, he was keen to get building. Ben had buried two children on the road, one of them his beloved grandson. As a result of that the child's parents had gone their separate ways but Ben had stayed, he'd begged his daughter not to go but she left regardless. And he was tired of being moved on by ruthless, uncaring people.

'Yes Mary, this will do nicely. We will build a solid foundation that will stand just about anything the mother can throw at it. One that you can build on. And by God we will build a house that will stand the test of time. No more children dying of the cold and starvation. That is the extent of what we owe you Mary.' Ben wiped a tear from his eye and smiled softly at Mary.

'Amen to that Ben' said Mary, a tremor in her voice. She'd grown fond of these people in the short time she'd known them.

Ben selected four posts, huge lengths of timber that it took two men to carry.

'We'll have to cart these home two at a time so's not to harm that lovely horse of yours Mary. These I would like to use for corner posts, and they will bear the brunt of the load. Then we will use your trees Mary and in between those some of these lesser timbers. We'll grab some of these beauties here for cross beams.' Ben was getting excited, and Dan smiled at the old man.

Several times that day they loaded up the cart with good solid timber, not all that pretty but good and solid wood. 'Cross beams' he said as he pointed to a length of wood and 'struts' as he pointed to another.

Onto their fourth load they were travelling back along the shire road from the dump to the town. It was about a half a mile from the dump to Mary's property. A band of men stepped out in front of them. 'What do we have here then?' James a council man asked.

Mary smiled down at him 'it's not obvious councilman James?

How much of this do you need me to explain to you?' The men chuckled.

'You got no call to be a smart mouth, Mary. Mary of the shanty, that's what they call ...'

'I am aware of what they call me councilman James and I am well aware of what they call you. And I know what all the girls at school call you to. Why don't you and your little friends go and hassle somebody else council man James. Maybe next time find someone who doesn't know what they call you. If you would just get out of my way, I'll be going.' The men on the cart laughed openly and so did some of councilman James's men.

The other men crowded around councilman James looking eager. Councilman James puffed out his chest but mostly his gut just got bigger. 'I'm afraid you are not allowed to take that junk onto council property.' His voice held spite as he positively gloated, a nasty smile on his face. He looked at Dan, 'and anyway, you're not going to be there long enough to put a saw to it.' He laughed heartily then realised he was laughing on his own.

Mary was smiling at him, how he hated the bitch, the do gooder bitch that she was. Making this scum think they were worth anything. Well, they had a surprise coming....

Mary spoke almost lazily now, 'I am not, I am taking it off council property. And I'm sorry but not surprised to hear that you are afraid.'

'What? So, where are you bloody taking it then?' James was becoming belligerent.

'I am taking it to my property with the help of my friends here. You going to try and tell me what I can and can't take to my place? Get out of the way James or I will run the hell over you. Does the mayor know you're out here harassing me? You remember how close he was to my dad. Does your Mumma know you're out even?' There was more chuckling even from the men at his back. James hated to admit it, but the mayor did watch out for Mary.

His face was scarlet now, he'd taken a direct hit and he didn't like it. James spat as he spoke. 'I'll get the police...... you need permission to be here.'

'No, I don't, I pay rates, get out of the way or I will run over you.'

Mary flicked the reins 'haa…. Haa. Walk on Lilly, right on over them.'

The men in the road moved out of the way. Mary knew she may have made an enemy they didn't need. She looked at Dan and he nodded.

On the next two trips they didn't see the men again. They had gotten enough timber for the build and Mary suggested they grab some of the corrugated iron. Some of the men could begin sorting and straightening it. Mary had brought a draw knife and planer to straighten and tidy the logs and timbers.

The next morning Mary arrived at a bit passed seven and the men were all ready. The tree loppers had twelve of the trees, trimmed and ready to use, a few others had them cut into lengths and some more youths had dug most of the holes to put them in. The long house would measure forty feet by one hundred and it would stand roughly twelve feet high. Enough room for everyone to get in out of the worst of the weather.

The camp had been moved to the trees near the gardens by the river, but far enough away that the children could play without trampling on it. Mary and the six men went to the dump expecting to be stopped but they were not. They got enough timber for the roof and the iron to put over it.

The third trip Mary suggested they get some of the slate and stonework. They got good floorboards and two pieces of solid iron. 'For the fireplace,' said Mary. The men walked most of the way back with the loads so the cart wouldn't be so heavy. After the fifth load Mary decided her horse had had enough for the day and turned her loose in the paddock.

They spent the rest of the afternoon digging the rest of the postholes and some started erecting the posts. On some of the trips they did to the dump they got the kids to hunt for nails or tacks and all the wire they could find and drag back. Mary had a huge store of these things, but she wanted to keep as much as she could.

By the next week the framework was up ready to start on the walls. They all worked hard and by the following week the walls were up. The roof was almost on, it was a quick job, but it would be warm and solid. It was a joint effort everyone worked hard but everyone though tired at the end of the day was happy. They had some of their self-respect back and a sense of security. It was home.

Mary had to speak to Iris, though her face glowed, she was still sick. 'Iris, I don't mean to upset you, but I would like to examine you. I am a medicine woman of sorts, and I will try to help you.'

'You can't love. I have a tumour and that is that. I went to a doctor some time ago and he said I have a lump in my stomach. It hurts around here' she said as she touched her lower stomach.

Mary knew that if a doctor had told her that then there probably wasn't much, she could do beyond pain relief. She had a lot of that stored away. 'I'm sorry Iris, I think you may be right. When the pain gets bad come to me and I can help you with that. I'm sorry I can't be more help.'

'Oh, love you have been the answer to our prayers. At least when I die, I'll know my kids have a roof over their heads and a healthy diet and I cannot thank you enough.' Iris studied the young woman, 'how old are you love?'

'Seventeen, I'll be eighteen in a few months.' Mary smiled.

Dan had watched Mary's face very carefully during her conversation with his wife. He'd felt a rush of sickness when he saw the disappointment replace hope on her face as Iris talked to her. So, it was true.

Three weeks after they had started the build, they finished it. In the middle of the front wall, they had a huge doorway and at one end at the side, another smaller door. They had put in two windows in the front and had made covers on simple hinges that they could open or close.

The first end, the biggest end, was to be for families, mostly a sleeping area. The family cubicles were petitioned off by hanging tarps and some with wooden panels. At the end of the sleeping area along the side wall they had made a sort of dormitory for the teenage girls and young single women. It contained eight beds. The children shared their parent's cubicle. The doors on the cubicles were old blankets or sheets or curtains and even old tarp hung across. It afforded a little privacy. In the daytime these curtain doors were left open to air the place.

In the middle was a kitchen area. It had a huge fireplace and a long table with stools that sat twenty so usually the men waited until last to eat or they sat outside or on the floor. There was large shelving beside the fire. They made more shelving on the other side of the kitchen area. All roughly made, all solid like the house. At the other end was an area for the single men to sleep. They didn't bother much with petitioning.

The two sleeping areas at the ends of the house had wooden floors, wood that had been worked and treated with pig fat and looked as good as new. In the middle of the house where the table, also wood, and a fireplace were, they had put the rough slate on the floor. It was lovely, it was a credit to them.

Mary arrived at eight o'clock in the morning. 'Good morning, Mary,' said Dan. The others nodded and hailed her.

'Good morning one and all' said Mary all business like. Some of the blokes groaned inwardly, they'd thought they would have had day off. But Mary stood and looking straight at Dan she said, 'how many shovels do we have?'

'Probably about six including yours Mary,' said Dan.

'Good' said Mary 'we need to dig two big holes. One I reckon about four by twelve by about eight feet deep. The other away from that on the side near the garden by the river, needs to be about ten by seven by seven deep. This one will need to be lined and have steps down into it.'

'What are these holes for Mary' asked Dan?

'The biggest will be for sewerage waste, so we'll have to put structures on them to sit in, I reckon about four but it's up to you. We probably should put that along the fence about five hundred yards away over to the west. Most of the wind here is from the other direction see. The other, over this side, that we will line, will be your cellar. We'll put it close to the river.'

Dan looked at the girl open mouthed, then 'I believe you are right Mary. We'll start on that shortly. Have a cuppa girl.'

She sat and had a cuppa with them, and they talked and some of the people there talked of the future for the first time in years. Dan pointed that out at one stage, and they all nodded and knew they were changed. All thanks to the young girl sitting drinking a cup of tea seemingly miles away.

Suddenly Mary was back. 'I don't see why you couldn't build small dwellings for yourselves to sleep in if you wanted to, what do you think Ben? Like lean to's off the side of the long hut.'

Ben was the master builder and had built three and four-story buildings. He nodded eagerly, 'you could use the wall of this building, she is certainly strong enough. But for now, as the winter is now upon us, we are probably better off sleeping inside here.' He grinned widely at Mary, 'and it's warm in here. Lovely and warm Mary.' He was overcome with emotions and hugged Mary. Mary laughed and hugged him back, she liked Ben.

———✦———

Within the week the holes were dug with four rough shelters over it. They simply made a framework of boards for the floor and put four holes in it and laid it across the trench. Next, they attached small cubicles of corrugated iron over this and put seats over the holes. The whole thing was done so that farther down the track they could simply dig another hole and refit the framework and the cubicles etc over this. The seats had covers on them so they could cut down on the smell as much as possible though the structures were about a hundred yards from the hut.

Mary smiled and told them she'd be back tomorrow that they needed to do the walls on the cellar. They covered the cellar with corrugated iron and then threw sand on the top. A trap door was attached, and the stairs were well made so as to get thing in and out a little easier. Tree branches were placed over the whole thing.

While some of them were digging and building some of the men and most of the women were harvesting vegetables. They had a bumper crop and by the end of the following week the cellar was done and almost full. They had gotten wooden boxes to store things in and harvested ten hessian bags of potatoes and more would be ready in a few weeks.

The older men built a smoke house and a place to salt meat so as to keep it as long as possible. The meat was strung up in a roughly made meat safe. Mary brought them milk every day. Some of the women had gotten busy pickling vegetables and drying them, Mary had brought them a flagon of wine vinegar she'd bought especially at the market. Some were cooked and stored in the cool of the cellar and others were sliced thinly and dried. Some men built rough shelving inside to put jars on.

Some of the single men had decided to build a dwelling at the front left-hand side of the building to live in. They put a fireplace in it. Only the old men, the married men, Wally, and Jack stayed inside. The longhouse had trees on each wall which afforded shade and protection from the wind. When they built, they disturbed as little as possible, and they were most glad of the thick bushes now.

On these long cold nights, the men poured a bucket of water over the lid of the cellar. Next morning some of the things were almost frozen. Mary worried about things going off in summer. Summer would be their worst time. They would have to dry a lot of their food, she decided they'd need a bigger smoke house. She brought them some materials of hers to get this started.

Mary had always bought up offcuts of cotton and linen and calico from the Indian hawkers who called in to see her hoping to unload them for a small fee. Her linen cupboard was full of it.

She collected duck and goose down from the neighbours and she had made several quilts. She had made pillows and sheets. Mary also had her father's collection of hessian bags; it was almost floor to ceiling.

It was a Sunday and Mary had stayed at home to catch up on some of her own work. She decided to clean out these cupboards and made up her mind to load most of her hoarding onto the cart. She took half of the hessian bags as well.

Mary was happy to have the camp people on the foot of her property, she had worried about people coming in that way and making off with her animals and anything else they needed. Now nobody would get through her gate without being seen. She also enjoyed their company she thought as she jogged along the track.

She gave the material to the women who were overjoyed. It was decided to make decent shirts and dresses for the children. Mary suggested that next year when they had nice clothes the kids could be enrolled to go to school. Some of the mothers openly cried tears of joy. 'Those who want to can attend church' Mary said eagerly. She had tears in her eyes to though she didn't know why.

She gave over the quilts and pillows and material for sheets.

Mary gave the hessian bags to the men. They were eager to show Mary that the older men had made good size wooden boxes for each family to keep their possessions in. And they all had a bed of sorts. The men used some of the calico and linen and bags to string up and curtain off each families sleeping area as well.

The toilets were covered well enough and far enough away to have no smells. It was decided that the ladies would use the two to the left and the men the two to the right.

'For the time being' said Dan, 'we could use the rest of these bags on our beds. They will keep the kids warm if we throw them over the top of their blanket.' Everyone including Mary agreed. The men looked happy and not quite so skinny. They were home, and they loved it. Some even talked about trying to find work.

Mary asked Dan if she could speak to him alone, so they went over by the gardens. 'Dan, I don't want to frighten you but if I was you I 'd have patrols round here of a night-time. That bastard James will try something. But if he sees the place is guarded, he'll stay away. He's not very brave. In fact, he's a spiteful little coward. There are some nice pieces of wood over by the cellar, you could easily make baseball bats for the kids, then carry them at night. And I might just add Dan that you never leave the camp without at least five men here. And at least travel away in pairs. Just until we are accepted here.'

Dan nodded and smiled, 'yeah you did stir him up a bit Mary. I was thinking the same thing myself. We have been keeping a lookout overnight. I saw you picking up those pieces of wood, do you never stop Mary? Never stop thinking and working things out?' He looked about him and swung back to her. 'You know I love it here Mary,

I feel as though we have gone from the destitute to the privileged overnight. I will do everything I need to do to keep it safe.'

Mary smiled, and her face relaxed, 'you could make some of them cricket bats and even some stumps. Next time I go to market I'll get them a ball.'

Dan looked at Mary for a time and Mary felt she knew what was coming. 'I saw you talking to Iris the other night Mary. How bad is it?'

'I can't Dan. Just talk to her.'

'And fall apart right in front of her. I think she's counting on me to be strong.'

Mary nodded; she was lost for words. 'Dan, it's …. Well, it's… Talk to her.'

'Can you just tell me how long? How long Mary?' Dan was hunched over as if he was expecting a blow.

'I think she may see Christmas but anything after that is up to the Gods Dan.' Dan stood his shoulders hunched and his fists balled at his sides. Mary leaned forward and touched one gently, 'talk to her Dan.'

Dan pulled her roughly into his arms and cried on her shoulder. Standing up straight he stepped away from her. 'I'm sorry.'

'Don't be Dan. Don't be. I know how hard it is.'

Dan turned and looked at the hut 'How long do you reckon she's known Mary?'

'Quite a while Dan, I'd say. I can't be sure though.'

'Is it cancer?'

Mary nodded; her heart ached for the man she had grown quite fond of. He reminded her of her father in a way.

'Where abouts is it, Mary?'

'It's in her stomach Dan.'

'And how does she know Mary?'

'Well apparently, she saw a doctor in the city. Must have been before you left.

He told her there was nothing he could do then. I'm so sorry Dan.'

Dan smiled at the girl and wondered again at the maturity and the intelligence of her. 'Thanks for being honest with me. I don't know why she has kept it from me for years Mary. But since she is so sick, I guess I will never know.' He looked at the long hut and back to Mary and said softly, 'and thankyou once again for all that you have done for us Mary and all that I have learned from you so far.'

Mary smiled, 'well we never stop learning Dan, not if we want to survive.'

Mary got home a bit late that night and went straight to see the animals. After turning Lilly loose, she checked them and was relieved that they were all okay and still had food and water. She needed to pay more attention to these animals.

The next morning after she'd milked the cow, she went out early and set up the plough and the harness, she needed to get her garden in order. She would need a few days to finish harvesting what was left in the garden and do some more seeding.

Next she went to check the cellar and was amazed at how much food was left in there. Most of it could go to the market next week. She and Dan had taken vegies to the last market at Mary's suggestion, and he had quite a bit to sell. Mary had suggested it after pointing out to him that they would have bags and boxes of vegetables go off. 'You could spare quite a few fish and rabbits to' she'd told him and watched the wonder of it wash over him.

At the market Mary noticed he had the same look of excitement on his face as she had seen on her fathers. Dad would have liked him she thought. When he counted his money and found he had made four pounds ten he was overwhelmed.

'Thank you Mary I have learned such a lot from you. Not just growing this and that is a pleasure in itself, but selling produce Mary, My produce you know, things that I have grown. And people pay me for it. And some say how nice it is and I feel proud of myself. I never had that driving a truck around all those years Mary.'

'Well Dan, not everyone can drive a truck, it's a skill Dan that I don't think I could do. Don't sell yourself short Dan.'

'Thanks Mary. And I owe it to you that I could build a damn house now if I had to. Who would have thought? No I love these markets Mary, it makes me want to go home and start digging.'

'Do it Dan, nobody's going to go crook if you go outside the boundaries a little. Colour outside the line Dan. I can see that you love this' she smiled and Dan's breath caught in his throat.

Chapter 4

Mary was as good as her word as usual and brought home three tennis balls for the kids from the town when she went for the mail. Some of the younger men got in on it and soon had a game of cricket going.

Mary asked Dan if she could speak with him. She always spoke to him on important matters. Apart from the fact that she liked him and felt comfortable talking to him, he had taken on the role of leader here. 'What do you want to talk to me about Mary?' He was always intrigued; he knew she didn't ask to speak to him unless it was important.

Mary, as usual ploughed right in. 'I have a business proposal for you. If I make these next four acres here available to you, do you think we could turn it in to a commercial crop and make some money? What say you?'

Dan was struck dumb, but an excitement had made its way into his gut the like of which he had not felt in a long time or maybe even never. He grinned and nodded, 'I can't see why not. What did you have in mind Mary? We have saved plenty of seeds and such.'

Mary smiled 'I rather thought maybe you could put an acre of vegies in and the remaining three acres of wheat. The way things are going the government will be looking for food. It's the one thing its population can't do without and with war a constant threat. We'd have to get started though Dan, it's already April. If we got stuck in, we could have it done in a couple weeks at the outside.'

Dan grinned widely and nodded enthusiastically, 'damn it Mary I don't see why not. Have you thought about the reaping?'

Mary nodded and grinned, 'we'll cross that bridge when we come to it. We'd have a few months to work that out. Let's just get their hay. So you are up for it Dan? Wanna have a go? There's money to be made Dan and lots of it, we'd split it down the middle. I found out the other day that wheat has gone up in price yet again so the more we can put in the better I say. We don't have to stop at three acres. Better get inside I guess; I need to go soon.'

She turned and walked away, and Dan watched her go. He couldn't get over it, a mere slip of a girl. But he had no doubt she was a woman. All woman to if he was any judge. He hadn't had any comfort from a woman in a very long time he thought wistfully. 'Oh hell' he admonished himself severely, even if he wasn't married, he was probably a good ten years older than her. He walked away, but not before his pulse had quickened and he felt an old familiar pull. He was pretty sure Jack had set his cap for her anyway.

They got started on the ploughing the next morning at six o'clock and by teatime they had one acre ploughed. Most of that acre was seeded. By the end of two weeks the whole four acres were done and they all had aching backs.

Three acres were wheat, and one was potatoes and turnips and pumpkin. The staples as Mary said.

Mary stayed for tea that night at the long house and when the meal was done, she said casually, 'who's for doing another two acres if the weather holds? I've still got two bags of good seed. Then I shall be away for a time as my own gardens need attention. I have to catch rabbits and fish to see me through.'

Dan looked at this girl who had given them so much, 'Oh Mary. How could we have been so thoughtless. You have given us so much and we neglect you. We'll get this next two acres done as you say and then I will come and help you. I guess Jack will help to.'

Dan had seen Iris lift her head and watch him when he said about helping Mary, so he'd hooked Jack in. Jesus, he thought was it obvious? He looked at her now and she had a strange smile on her face. Oh, hell he didn't want to think about any of it.

His Iris was dying, he knew it and when Mary had told him this he hadn't been surprised. Hell, he thought, how long had he known? They had two boys he'd have to look after on his own and he knew nothing about that. Dan had always been a truck driver until he was made redundant like so many others. And Iris to be cut down in the prime of her life. He looked away from her. Dan got up and walked over to the fire to warm himself a shiver had passed through him on its way to his soul.

Mary had noticed it and she looked hard at Iris. The older woman was in pain, Mary would need to talk to her. Most of the blokes and some of the women had offered to come and help her get her garden sorted. Mary stood up to go, it was dark out already. 'Just a few of you will do. And thank you very much, now I will see you around seven in the morning.'

Dan stood up and winked at his wife, 'I'll come with you for a way just in case our friend James is out already. Come on Jack, you to Wally.' He turned to Ben and indicated he come. At the door he asked Ben to organise the first watch outside.

They took Mary all the way home and jumped down from the cart. Dan told Jack to go in and help Mary get the light going and the fire started while he and Wally unharnessed the horse.

Jack got the fire going while Mary lit the light. He looked around at her hut. It was clean and tidy and very homely, but it wasn't flash. Everything she had looked comfortable and plain. He liked it. He asked her if she needed any help fishing and catching rabbits.

Mary smiled 'I may do Jack, so I hope you meant that. The paddocks are important though. First heavy rain we won't be able to plough. I checked with Mavis at the post Office, and she says there is no rain forecast for the next few days anyway. We have been lucky the heavy rains are late this year. We'll get them done I think and if we get them done you should look at getting another one done. That would be six acres of wheat and who knows if the rain holds off. And if some of the older guys got busy on more vegies it should bring in a bit of cash for your community. So, I hope you are ready for yet more work Jack' she smiled now.

Jack was always dumb struck when she smiled at him. 'Oh, of course I am Mary, I hope you'll call on me anytime you need a bit of help.' He stared at her;

he couldn't help it. 'I.... I....'

The door was flung open, and Wally, a strapping young man in his early twenties and around six foot two walked in with Lilly and took her through where Mary showed him. 'You are certainly not going to let anyone pinch her Mary' he smiled.

'I couldn't do without her Wally' she said.

He nodded and smiled looking back at Lilly, 'she has certainly saved our bacon, her and you Mary.'

Dan was in the kitchen and said they best get going. 'It's at least a half hour walk gentlemen.' He smiled at Mary.

On the way back Jack talked excitedly of the next two acres they were going to put in. Dan and Wally had loaded the two bags of seed on the cart ready for tomorrow to save Mary having to do it. Dan, as he walked quietly along beside the youngster, was wondering about the young man's intentions towards Mary, he hoped they were honourable. Knowing Jack as he did, they probably would be.

———⟶⟶⟶⟶⟵⟵⟵⟵———

The men were all up, eaten and standing around outside talking excitedly.

'What's the time Ben' asked Dan?

Ben took his watch out of his pocket and studied it, 'Shit it's eight o'clock Dan. I wonder what's up? She is never this late.'

Dan had a bad feeling in his stomach. It was growing by the minute. 'I'm going to start walking to her hut. You come with me Ben, the rest of you get out to the paddock there.'

Along the road Ben said to Dan 'you think somethings happened to her Dan?'

'I dunno Ben I hope not,' They'd walked about a halfway when they heard a horse and cart coming. The two men stopped and waited as the girl came into view. Dan's heart lurched in his chest as he saw the state of her face. One of her eyes was blackened and she had a split lip.

'Good morning, how are you?' The two men stared. 'Sorry I'm late I slept in.' Mary offered no other explanation.

'Your face….' Began Dan.

'Get in Dan, you to Ben.' Keeping her eyes to the front she clicked to Lilly, and they were off. She said quietly, 'I had a little visit from some of councilman James' little friends. To cut a long story short I gave them all a good hiding with that whip I bought for Lilly. You know I had always hoped I'd fine a use for it; I would never use it on Lilly but the man in the shop told me I needed it. I got these bruises because I let them sneak up on me. Well anyway Jim kept them busy while I made it outside. And there on the veranda was the very thing I needed to convince them that they suddenly wanted to be at home with their wives.'

'Are you alight Mary? Your face…. Those bastards! This is because of us Mary.

Oh Mary….'

'I'm alright thanks. It's all over Dan, none of it is your fault, I want you to remember that. I knew he'd revisit me, but he lacked the intestinal fortitude to come alone and do his dirty work. I told you he was a cowardly little man. But I let the bastards sneak up on me. I thought I was smarter than that.' Mary clicked to Lilly to hurry on a bit. 'Anyway, we've got work to do. Dan if it's alright with you I'll do today, and you can drop me off home tonight with Lilly and take her back with you and I'll spend a couple of days at home.'

'Alright Mary, are you okay to work? We can do it Mary.' Dan's voice shook with emotion, Ben was having trouble with his emotions.

Mary went on quickly, 'I just need to stick close to home for a while. Dan don't relax your guard on your home and your families for a minute. When you're at work leave at least a few strong men home to guard them and remember the value in old heads when you do. Your families are more important than the bloody crops though the vegie gardens are pretty important to. I will get you a young dog from one of the neighbours. He'll let you know when anybody's about and the kids will love him.'

Dan smiled and nodded 'sounds good Mary, we probably should think about watching the crops at night. You're right, we do need those vegies to, else we'd be in for a fairly lean winter, and we can't keep living off you Mary. We've kept quiet about our cellar Mary, so no one knows it's there.'

'Good Dan' Mary smiled.

At the long house, the men stared at Mary in horror and so did the women. Their hero, their saviour… hurt! Who could have done this? Mary refused a cuppa, 'we have lost enough time thanks to me.' And Mary worked the whole day and never complained. She even took her turn at the plough. It nearly broke Dan's heart.

As the sun was nearing the horizon and the men were getting ready to have tea Mary said she had to go. 'If someone wants to come with me to bring Lilly back to pull the plough tomorrow.'

'Go on Jack' said Dan, 'and have a good look round when you get there. Stay with Mary tonight and come back in the morning.'

Mary smiled at Dan; she would be glad of Jack tonight. 'Thanks' she said, 'do you mind Jack?'

'Course not.' He turned and said goodbye to Dan.

Dan winked at him and said 'stay alert boy. We need you and so does your country.' Jack blushed and turned to Mary.

Lilly had pulled the plough all day, so Mary and Jack walked beside her.

As they got along the road Jack said 'Mary did they …. Did……?'

'No. Jack let's not talk about it anymore.'

'Okay Mary. But I'm glad all the same.'

———ᴡᴡ∘ᴄᴇᴛᴏᴄᴛᴇᴏ∘ᴡᴡ———

With Mary pushing them, the men got the two acres done in just over a week. The next day the heavens opened up and the rain poured down. Jack jumped out of bed hearing the rain on the roof. Dan was already at the door and turned to smile at the young man. 'Raining cats and dogs' he said looking back up at the sky.

'Good for the crops and the garden' Jack said and headed off to get some coffee, a big smile on his face. Things were looking up he thought.

They hadn't seen Mary for a couple of days and Dan planned

to go and check on her this morning, he had to take the horse back anyway. They had worked out a signal if Mary got into trouble and needed them. She was to fire the 22rifle three times into the air.

The older men had got to work the last couple of days and built a lean-to veranda and put down left over slate stones from the build for the floor, and a scraping board for their boots. It was rough but it kept the rain off and the doorway dry and the men could leave their dirty boots outside. Kept the floors clean and the women happy.

Two of the younger men, Dennis, and Ron, had gotten hired on to work on the railways. 'We start Monday, will that be alright Dan? We just thought, you know, with the work mostly done we could make some money for extras like.'

They told Dan they would donate their wages to the community which was home to them now and had saved their lives.

Dan had accepted and thanked them in a somewhat shaky voice. 'You keep some for yourselves' he'd told them clapping them on the shoulder. 'Well done lads.' This praise from the big man was everything to Dennis and Ron who idolised him.

When Jack had his coffee, he went and sat at the table with Dan. He leaned forward and after briefly searching the older man's face, he asked respectfully if he could talk to him about something.

Dan nodded and smiled at the young man he'd come to respect. 'Course you can Jack. You know you don't need to ask mate.'

Jack looked down at the table and with eyes fixed firmly on the coffee cup he began. 'See Dan, I applied to join the army a few weeks ago and I believe they have sent my draft papers.' Jack pulled an envelope from his pocket and laid it on the table in front of Dan.

Dan looked at Jack's face and though he knew Jack could read Dan thought the papers were probably a bit much for him. 'Can I have a look, Jack' he asked softly?

Jack nodded dumbly and watched as Dan read the papers. Jack had told no one he'd applied but he had waited until he saw the end to their work in sight. Still, he held his breath, the approval of the older man was very important to him.

Finally, Dan looked up and smiling he said 'yes indeed Jack, you have been accepted. Are you happy about this?'

Jack shrugged, 'I am Dan. I'm not sure when I'm supposed to report or where.'

Dan looked down at the papers, a frown making its way across his handsome features. 'Jack' he said slowly, gently. 'You are to report in just over a months' time. On the twentieth of June. You are to go to Melbourne, Jack. To the Victoria barracks out on St Kilda Road. Do you know where that is Jack?'

Dan looked across the table at the young man, and for some reason he couldn't fathom his heart ached. He stood to lose too many people, first his dad and Iris and now Jack. Dan suspected war was coming, how could he bear it? Jack, going to war. Then again, he thought sadly, most of the younger men would probably be called up.

Jack noted the look on the big man's face and smiled brightly, 'don't worry Dan, they couldn't kill me with an axe.' Jack dropped his head and wiped his eye. Looking back up at Dan he said 'I'll miss you Dan. But at least if I do go to war, I'll know you and your families will be fine.' Jack sniffed and picked up his cup and downed his coffee.

'Have you told Mary any of this?'

'No, I thought it best to wait and see. You know.' After a pause he went on 'In the event that something happens to me look out for her Dan. I know you will man. You all will, we owe her so much.' Jack sniffed and dropped his voice so no one would hear. 'How is Iris Dan?'

Dan shook his head as much in surprise as anything, 'she's…. uh… Well do you know how to get to Victoria barracks or don't you?' Dan smiled sadly at the young man. 'And how are you gunna get there?

'Well, I'll bloody walk Dan. You can draw me a map. I'll remember it, you just draw it and I'll remember it.'

It was too much for Dan and a tear slid down his cheek, so he rose abruptly out of his chair and walked outside. Jesus, he asked himself, why had things to hurt so bloody much. Of all the blokes, why did it have to be Jack? Dan was so certain there was war coming to them.

'He told you then?'

Dan swung around and looked into the wizened, weather-beaten old face of Ben. He nodded, 'yeah he told me Ben.'

'He was worried you wouldn't take it well Dan, and with good reason I see.'

Ben reached out and took Dan's arm in a firm grip as he looked steadily up into the face of his leader. A man he had come to admire very much and smiled kindly. 'And at such a time Dan.'

Dan lowered his head and, in a voice, just above a whisper he said, 'at such a time, Ben.'

Chapter 5

*I*t was early evening, and the camp was getting ready to eat. It had rained for a week and had stopped a few hours ago. The sun had come out that afternoon and the women were preparing to wash the next day down at the river. The men had rigged up a drum over a fire and this they would use as a copper.

Some of the men had built a lean-to at the back of the long house and put a bath in it. It was an old claw foot bath that they had rescued from the dump and made a wooden plug for it. Jack had been in for a scrub; he was off to see Mary. His stomach was churning at the thought of it, he hadn't seen her for two days.

Jack shaved and was dressed in his best pants and his only clean shirt. Ben walked up to him and handed him a bottle. Jack looked into his smiling face and took the aftershave. He applied a little to his face and handing it back he thanked Ben and left by the side door.

Jack walked the quarter mile at a brisk pace, he wanted to get there before dark. His mind was in a quandary, what would Mary think of him going off to join the army at such a time? And should he tell her how he felt about her? He had spent quite a bit of time in her company and had come to feel comfortable with her. But what if she rejected him, what then? Well, he mused, he'd be leaving in just on a month so he wouldn't have to be around making them both awkward for long.

He walked as fast as he could his head bowed in thought. Suddenly he was afraid, afraid he wouldn't be able to leave Mary. Maybe it would be best if she did reject him. He shook his head; he didn't believe that.

'Good evening, Jack.'

Jacks head came up and he looked about him. And there emerging from the bush, as if from a fairy tale, was his Mary. He watched her walk towards him, he was speechless, how he loved her. She smiled at him.

'Hello Mary, I came to see you.'

'Good Jack, that's where I was going. Can I walk with you?' She walked past him a bit.

Jack made a now or never decision and grabbed her gently by the wrist and stopped her. He took her hand in his and walked beside her, hand in hand. Mary smiled at him, and Jack felt his taught muscles relax a little. He couldn't believe she'd accepted him. Just like that. Jack walked on air all the way to Mary's shanty. All too soon they were at her door, and he had to let go of her hand. He stepped to the side to let her go in.

'Sit down Jack, do you want a coffee?'

Jack nodded, he swallowed deeply and watched her go about the kitchen. When they were sat at the table Mary looked into his troubled face and all the longing there and smiled. 'What is it Jack' she asked?

Jack stared at her, at the loveliness of her and it nearly broke his heart. 'I'm going away Mary' he said and watched the light in her eyes fade.

'Jack' she was trying to smile but knew it wasn't happening. 'Jack' she said again and could only gape at him. She never would have expected this. Finally, she said 'where are you going Jack' in a tiny voice?

'Mary, I joined up. I'm going into the army. I have to be in Melbourne in a month. I wish I could take it back Mary. I need to earn money for the community as we call it, for my family. I should have checked with you though Mary. You have come to mean a lot to me Mary.'

Jack watched in horror as tears appeared in her eyes and rolled down her cheeks. She got up abruptly from the table and went to go passed him to her room. She was going to cry. But she had to hold back, at least till she made it to her room. Damn you Jack, she thought bitterly.

She couldn't see properly for the tears and her throat and chest were hurting so much it hurt to breath. Suddenly Jack was in front of her, and she was in his arms. He pulled her to him and held her gently. The dam burst and Mary sobbed, great sobs that wracked her body. She wasn't sure why she just did.

When she had cried the worst of the pain out, she looked up at him and noted the tears running down his own cheeks. She reached up and wiped them away with her hands. 'Oh Mary' he croaked. When his lips came down on hers, he felt a most wondrous feeling. And when Marys arms went round him his head swam. She kissed him fiercely for a moment and Jack kissed her back with equal passion.

'Mary, I need you' he murmured. She held him tighter. Jack picked the girl who had stollen his heart up in his arms and took her to her room. Mary murmured his name into his neck which was still wet with their tears.

In the dark of Mary's room Jack kissed her tenderly and they clung to each other. Out of their misery was born a great love. Oddly enough, Mary knew, she could only hope to find solace in the arms of the man who had brought her such misery. Yet he had brought her such love to, and she had never imagined such a feeling.

'Mary I will get leaves and I will come home to you. I love you with all my heart and I want to marry you.' He kissed her again and she responded not quite as enthusiastically. Mary had a feeling that anything which may have been born between the two of them might now be doomed.

Jack stayed with her and they talked until she lay sleeping. He got up off the bed and went to head home. She stirred and sat up and he kissed her gently on the lips. 'Go back to sleep my love and I will be back at first light. I promise darling. I'll be back for more of this, you can be sure of that.' He chuckled deep in his throat, and she kissed him and went back to sleep. 'You be here Jack.'

Jack walked home in a daze; he had just made love to the most beautiful woman on the planet. Jack had never been in love before and as he walked the quarter mile, he let the tears rain down his face. How he loved her. How could he leave her? 'Oh Mary' he whispered into the cold dark night, 'my Mary. What have I done?'

When Jack reached home, everyone was sleeping, and he went to the kitchen. The tea in the pot was almost cold but it would do. He took his cup of tea outside and sat on one of three logs they all used as an outdoor setting. His head was still swimming, and a smile made its way across his face. Mary loved him, she loved him, and how good it felt. He was suddenly aware that someone had sat down beside him on the log. He turned and smiled at Dan.

'Well lad? You told her?'

Jack nodded his head slowly.

'How did she take it Jack?' Dan asked softly.

'She cried Dan, I made her cry. Blast me for a fool, I made her cry.' Jack hung his head and wiped his eyes and nose.

Dan could find nothing to say to ease his young friend, no words of comfort came to him. He slid closer and put his arm across Jacks shoulders and held him firmly as he gave a sob. 'You had your first experience with love tonight, Jack? Most blokes get a bit emotional after just such an occasion. But at least you told her how you feel. Didn't you?'

Jack nodded and smiled distantly. 'Yeah, I did, I told her I love her, and she loves me back. Jesus Dan, she is one hell of a woman. I must be the luckiest bloke alive.' He sniffed.

Dan hugged him and said he was happy for him. 'I hate to be a wet blanket Jack but are you going across there tomorrow lad?'

Jack nodded, 'I am supposed to be there at first light, she has some work for me to do. Why Dan?'

'Mate, could you ask her to come and see Iris when she can? Just whenever, you know.'

'Shit Dan is Iris worse? I'm sorry Dan, I'm sorry to bring all this to you on top of everything you are going through. I'll get her here tomorrow, Dan, you can count on it.'

'Thanks lad. These are bad times we are living through you know, but they are going to get so much worse.' Dan patted Jack on the back as you would a squalling toddler. 'The love of a good woman will be a comfort to you when the time comes Jack. Let it be a comfort to you lad.' Jack turned and hugged his best friend. He knew men didn't do that but to hell with it, he'd had a big day and he loved the big guy.

When Mary approached Iris' bed, she could smell the sickness. She stood and looked at Dan and back at Iris. The woman was thin and pale, and she was also asleep. She motioned Dan to follow her outside. They sat on the log, and everyone left them be. It was a great sadness amongst them, what was happening to their dear friend Iris. She was family and she suffered greatly.

Somebody brought them a coffee each and left again.

'She has gone downhill remarkably Dan' Mary stated sadly, her heart breaking for the big man she'd come to respect above all others. Mary realised she had never been anything but glad she'd come to know him. But Dan had hung his head, his misery apparent.

Mary reached into her coat pocket and brought out a package of the herbs she'd been giving Iris for the pain. 'Dan, Iris' cancer is apparently very aggressive now. I am sorry to my core to say this Dan, but all we can do now is try to make her comfortable. Did I hear that one of the men's wives here had been a nurse?'

Dan raised his eyes to Marys and marvelled at the love and compassion in them. Yes, he thought now, maybe Jack really was the luckiest man in the world after all. He nodded dumbly to her knowing he dare not open his mouth lest the floodgates be opened and remain open.

Mary nodded her head in understanding for his plight and went on gently.

'Good, we are going to need a nurse. Can she be in on this conversation Dan?'

Dan nodded his head.

When Dennis' wife Noreen was sat with them at the long table Mary asked her if she had actually been a registered nurse. The woman nodded and Mary heaved a sigh of relief. Jack walked up and sat next to Mary, he had to know.

Mary took a small vial from her coat pocket and handed it to Noreen. The older woman took it turning it over in her hand she looked up at Mary, 'has it come to this already?' Her look was pleading, and Mary found it difficult to keep a stiff upper lip.

She nodded slowly to the woman and turning to Dan she said gently, 'it is morphine Dan. These pain relievers I have been giving her aren't even taking the edge off now. This will relieve most of her pain, but she will sleep a lot.

Maybe you will see only a few hours a day with her, maybe more, but we have no alternative that I can see.'

She looked at Noreen and Noreen nodded her agreement before turning to Dan. 'She's right Dan. Iris is in a bad way love. The pain must be bloody bad by this.'

Dan sniffed and wiped his eyes and nose. Jack got up and went and sat next to him and put his arm across his shoulders. 'I'm sorry mate' he said in a shaky voice.

Mary went on and though Dan wished she would not he made himself sit still. 'Do you agree to us administering morphine Dan? We have enough here to make her next two weeks comfortable. At the end of that time, I can go and get more. If you would rather a doctor, make a decision here Dan I will get one, I don't mind, and I can afford it. As I see it Dan...' Mary drew a shaky breath and put her hand on Dans, 'this is our only ace to play, we're out of options. I am heart sorry Dan. So, heart sorry.'

She watched Dan wipe furiously at a tear before he spoke. His voice was low and painfilled, 'I know what you say is true Mary. It's just....'

Noreen butted in now, 'we would administer it sublingually Dan, it would cause her no pain, we just put the drops under her tongue, I think twice a day. It won't kill her Dan, won't end her life any sooner it will just improve her quality of life while she lives. She may even be able to get up and go outside And Lord knows it matters little if she gets addicted.'

Dan looked at Mary, she nodded and waited for him to speak. Then she said softly 'I'll wait for your decision Dan; I don't want to push you on this. I'll wait all day Dan, if need be, I will be here. When we administer the drug Noreen will be here to oversee her. Won't you Noreen?'

'Of course.'

Dan looked at Jack and raised his eyebrows. Jack wiped snot from his nose and hugged his mate 'I think we should buddy. If Iris can just get some peace from all this pain, she's in.' Jack ended on a sob. He was a mess and not much help at all thought Noreen.

Noreen touched Dans arm and said gently, 'we can't save her love. She's going to die; we all know that, and she knows that.'

Dan looked at Mary and holding her gaze he nodded, 'alright Mary. I hate seeing her suffering the way she is. I don't mean to be uncaring, it's just that I am her sole advocate now. You, see?'

Mary smiled and took both Dans hands in hers and squeezed them, 'and if I were in her position, I wouldn't be able to wish for a better advocate to have in my corner. You have done this just right Dan; you got all the facts and gave it a deal of thought before you came to a decision. And for what it's worth I think you have made the right decision and you did it with love. We are all here for you Dan, we all owe you a lot.'

The dam burst and Dan cried unashamedly and unabashed. Hands came out and held him firm in their love for him. Most of the people there were crying to.

When he was through Mary asked Noreen about the dosage and the method of administering the drops. 'Will this do' she asked producing an eye dropper. 'I have cleaned if thoroughly.'

Noreen took the eyedropper 'this is fine thanks Mary' and withdrew a few drops of the precious liquid. Going to Iris she found the woman awake.

Dan arrived and sat beside the bed staring at his wife. 'I'm sorry Dan' she said, 'I know I have been a trial to you.'

'Oh, don't be silly dear' he said gently. 'Listen my dear, Noreen here is going to give you some medicine which will greatly ease your pain.' He smiled tenderly at the woman who had given him two sons.

Iris looked at Noreen and the nurse said to her dear friend, 'I am going to put some drops of this under your tongue. It may make you feel a bit queasy at first and you might go off to sleep. But you'll gradually get used to it and find it very beneficial.'

'Thanks Noreen'. She looked at Mary now, 'and thank you Mary. Thank you for having the guts to step up and take matters in hand

and thank you for bringing this medicine. And while I'm on I 'd like to thank you for the fact that me and my family and friends here all eat well and are warm and cosey from the stark winter. We are home because of your generosity Mary, and we are settled for the first time in a long while. And we have you to thank that I am the only one dying here.'

It brought Mary undone and crying, her knees buckled as she knelt and put her arms gently around the woman on the bed and spoke softly, lovingly. 'If you will open your mouth my dear friend, we can get these drops in and working. I will stay with you and so will Noreen and Dan. You'll be okay, no more of this terrible pain. No more of it, Iris.'

When the drops had been administered, they all stood around holding their breath, Mary still holding Iris' hand. A few minutes afterwards, Iris visibly relaxed and she breathed a great sigh.

'Oh, thank you, thank you Mary. I have not felt this good in years. Thank you, Dan thank you.' She put her hand out and held his. 'I don't know how you did it Dan but thanks.' She smiled and asked her husband if she could see her boys.

'It's been so long since I was able to hug them and kiss them. Please Dan.'

A wide grin found its way across his handsome face and brought with it a pain to Iris' heart that there was no medicine for. She watched him hurry off.

———— ᴡᴏᴏᴄᴇᴛᴏᴏᴛᴇᴏᴏᴡ ————

Later that day when the evening meal was done, and Mary had spent a couple of hours with Iris and was satisfied that she was much improved for the medication, she told Jack she would go home and left the hut. He stood up and followed her outside. He said, 'alright Mary I'll just say Tatar to….'

Mary put her hand on his arm and smiled up at him. 'Not tonight my love, stay for Dan. He is bewildered. He looks to you for comfort and takes his que from you, today anyway. Putting Iris on morphine…. Well though he sees it makes her better it is the dead finish, and he knows it. Stay love, just tonight. I love y...' Mary's voice was cut off when she was pulled into his arms. His mouth came down on hers hard and a sob escaped him. Her arms went around him and brought him a feeling he couldn't get over.

He let her go 'I will be there at first light Mary my darling and I hope to not bring bad news. I'd like to thank you Mary for always being there and for saving us. And most of all thank you for finding it in your heart to love me.' He looked down at this woman with wonder in his face.

Dan watched the exchange from inside the hut. How he wished he could talk to her for a short while, but he couldn't intrude. He felt a weight of gratitude for the girl and vowed he'd do anything for her. He would give anything to be held in her arms that way, just for an instant. 'Oh God' he whispered and lowered his head.

Disgusted with himself, Dan turned to go back inside. He didn't see the tear- filled eyes that had watched and understood what was in the big man's heart. 'Dear Lord' the old man said to himself and turned back to the fire. Ben got up slowly from his chair and got himself a cuppa to help him try and digest the great sadness's of this day which had formed as a lump in his throat. Who could help falling in love with Mary anyway? The tears fell, he cried for Iris, and he cried for her husband, a man with a heart that was just too big.

Jack came back in, and Dan asked him why he hadn't gone with Mary. 'I just wanted to be here Dan. I want to be with her to but, you and Iris…. You took me in Dan, you know you did. I hope she gets some good times in before…. Oh bugger!'

Jack couldn't believe he'd been so stupid. He heard a chuckle and looked up.

Dan walked to the fire, 'come and sit-down boy, Iris is asleep now anyway.' Jack sat down, 'I'm sorry.'

'You meant well Jack, you always do mate, and you're spot on. She hugged the boys and kissed them and had a good talk with them today for the first time in so long. Thanks for being there for us Jack. I owe you mate.'

Dan settled himself down at the table before going on, 'Jack, you know Dennis and Ron want to pay your train fare to Melbourne, so you won't have to leave three days early. Mary is going to see about getting permission to bury Iris here, you know, down by the river. You are lucky Jack. Just be happy man, even when you go away, you'll still have her here waiting for you. No…. be happy lad you deserve it.'

'It's a bad bloody time to be running off. I'm sorry Dan but I don't think I can change it can I?

Dan looked up into Jacks face at the beseeching there and swallowed. He shook his head; 'I don't think so lad. But when you get to Melbourne see what you can do if you have a mind to. Maybe on compassionate grounds or something.'

Ben sat at the table with the two men who had come to be family members to him. He wanted to listen to these two men, had to make sure all was right between them. Running true to form the two men had put their friendship above everything else for the good of everyone. Ben breathed a sigh of relief, so much depended on the relationship between these two working.

The three men talked, for a while and Iris woke up. Noreen, it had been decided would give Iris another dose of morphine after she'd tried to eat and drink. To everybody's surprise Iris ate a plate of food and drank half a glass of milk. Dan felt himself relax. He had done right; he was pretty sure he had. For once in his miserable life, he had done right by his Missus.

Dan sat by her side for a little while before getting up to take the dishes to the kitchen and wash them up. Iris watched him go and marvelled at the feelings she still had for him. She had loved him from the moment she set eyes on him twelve years ago.

Iris considered herself to be the happiest woman on earth the day she married Dan Roberts. She'd let Dan take liberties, unable to find it in herself to stop him, and had become pregnant at nineteen years of age.

The only blot on her bright world was the fact he had married her because he felt he had to. That was the sort of man he was. Iris overlooked the women he'd had on the side. But how she had loved him and so had taken what she could get from him. And he had been a good husband and a good father. And even though she had lost that first baby, he had stuck by her.

She lay in her bed clean and warm and thanked God's mercy that she had little pain and was tired. So tired. Vaguely she heard Dan come back to their sleeping area and hop into bed with their youngest boy. 'Dan' she whispered.

He got up and sat on the side of her bed, 'what is it dear are you in pain?'

'No Dan, not very much' she lifted the covers for him to get in. He sat back gazing at her. 'Just this one last time Dan. Please baby, then I can die happy.

Just love me one last time.'

Dan lay himself gently down beside her and took her gently in his arms.

'Oh Dan.'

Chapter 6

*J*ack sat in the odd-looking chair beside Iris' bed and said goodbye to her. The day had come for him to leave. He put his arms gently around the woman and she hugged him to her. 'Oh Jack, come back to us lad. I will miss you and so will Dan and the boys. I can't bear the thought I might never see you again.'

'Oh hush, Iris' Jack cried, 'I'll be back soon when I get some leave. I was talking to an old fulla in at the railway yards the other day when I was waiting for Dennis and Ron to knock off so's I could walk home with them. Well, he got out of the army 'bout thirty years ago and he reckons they give you a couple weeks leave when you finish your basic training. In about two or three months. I'll be seeing you, Iris. Alright?'

'Alright love if you say so.' She smiled weakly at him and as ever was grateful she could say goodbye to him.

Jack planted a kiss on her cheek and grinned at her even though his heart was breaking. He heard Mary pull up on the horse and a sink hole opened up in the pit of his belly. He kissed Iris again and went to the door where all his stuff was waiting. He had a small kaki bag which he had everything he owned in and a jacket.

Everyone except Iris and her nurse Noreen and a couple of babies went with him to see him off. All on foot, some barefoot, all straggling down the road and through the town. The children all crowding around their beloved hero Jack. All wanting to touch him.

And Jack had never looked so breathtakingly nor devastatingly handsome to Mary as she walked arm in arm by his side. On the platform, Jack stood holding Mary close to him after he'd said his goodbyes. 'Write to me Mary. I'll write to you and send my address. I don't write very well Mary, but I'll do my best.' Mary smiled and kissed him. When he heard the train coming, he was almost relieved, this was killing him. He kissed Mary and stepped into the carriage.

Closing the door, he turned to look at the motley bunch he had for a family now and tears rained down his cheeks. He loved them one and all. Dennis and Ron weren't there, they'd had to work but Jack had thanked them before they went, for his train ride.

'Well, it beats walking Jack.' Ron had laughed pressing a two-bob piece into his hand. 'Get yourself some lunch mate. We are all proud of you buddy.'

Dennis looked steadily at Jack for a moment and said 'Jack, by the way things are looking we will be down there beside you afore long. If they do what I hear around about and bring back conscription. So, keep us a good bunk hay?'

The two men embraced Jack and left for work. At the doorway Ron had looked back and said, 'leave one or two sheilas for me will ya Jack.' The three men laughed.

The train began puff puffing, gathering steam for take-off. As the train gave a jerk and slowly set off down the track Jack leaned out the window and screamed. 'Mary... Mary, wait for me?'

Mary took his hand and walked along the platform tears streaming down her face. 'Oh Jack of course I will.'

'And get that paperwork organised darlin.' He grinned as best he could.

'Yes Jack, Oh yes.' She had to let him go. Her hand was pulled from his and she cried out 'Jack, Jack!'

Mary stood on the platform sobbing and then she felt a strong arm go round her. Dan helped her to watch Jack disappear from sight. She turned to him, and he held her gently as she sobbed. Long after the train had disappeared, and everyone turned their backs Dan got his one and only wish. Mary buried her face in his neck and wrapped her arms around him.

He marvelled just then at the fact, when life could be so bad for the one yet it was so good for the other. Why he asked his saddened heart? Why had his wishes to wear such a price tag?

———✦———

In the weeks that followed Jacks leaving, life got back to the daily grind. The men left at home would tend the gardens in the daytime and do general maintenance. Wally got a part time job at the local store. He donated most of his wage to Dan to be used for the community.

It pleased the people of the community and lifted their spirits to be so accepted into the township. Though people didn't mix much yet with them at least they didn't regard them with so much suspicion. Jack sent home most of his army pay. The community had never been so well off, they had money now. And it was largely thanks to Dan and the loving way he managed the place. Everyone just knew, if Dan said or did something, it was fair and just.

Dan watched with fascination as the brown paddocks became green with the wheat they had sewn. He would smile when he thought how happy it made him to just stand still and watch the grass grow. The weather was kind to them and was raising a bumper crop. They had strung a fence across to keep Marys' animals out of it.

Mary climbed down off her horse; she would visit with Iris today. Iris was mostly unaware of her surroundings now. Mary had got the doctor out to see her and he had told them that all he could do was to keep them in a supply of the merciful pain killing fluid that they were using. However, Noreen was given a tin box with lock and key to keep it in.

The mayor himself had written permission for them to bury the woman on the property providing it was overseen by the city mortician or funeral director. He would satisfy the mayor, in writing, that everything was done according to public health regulations.

Mary had a local carpenter make her a nice coffin, from the red river gums that Dan loved so much, which she had kept at her place. The man had polished it to a high sheen and lined it with good white linen. When she told Dan he had thanked her and shaking his head 'what would we do without you Mary?'

She undid the bag from the saddle horn now and left Lilly to munch some grass. Jack had been gone for almost two months and Mary found these trips to the community helped her a lot. A thought kept nagging at her concerning Jack. It was as if something was telling her she'd just best get over him. She loved these visits with Dan, she knew they both needed them.

She turned to walk into the long hut and smiled when she saw Dan. He watched her walk towards him. She held up the bag 'I have something for you Dan. I think you'll like it. I got it from a travelling hawker for a song.' She refused his help with it, shrugging him off. Dan scratched his head.

Inside, Mary plopped the bag on the table. She had to use both hands to remove the content from the bag as it was fairly large and heavy. Dan stood staring, dumbfounded, at the object she had just plonked on the table. He walked slowly towards it. Putting his hands lovingly on the radio he whispered, 'for me Mary?' He turned wide eyes on her, 'it can't be Mary. Do you know how I have wished for one of these? Well of course you do....'

Mary laughed and told him 'Now you can keep up with whatever is going on in the world Dan.' Mary knew Iris had days left at best and the strain was taking its toll on the big man.

Mary asked him where he wanted it, but he could only stare. Finally, he raised his eyes to hers and stated simply 'I could listen to the news Mary. Think on it.' He straightened his shoulders and stared at it then running his hands over it he sat at the table. He ran his fingers over the dog and the horn, 'His Masters Voice no less Mary. The very best.... For me.'

'Okay Dan, we'll leave the thing here on the table for now. I have brought you some wire in case you need to set up an aerial. I need one for mine when there's bad weather about. Turn it on Dan.'

Dan turned a knob; Mary knew it would work because she'd had it going even before she bought it. The radio squealed into life and a man's voice came to them loud and clear giving the weather for the next day. Mary turned to look at Dan and was moved by the tears running down his tired and haggard face. He looked a good ten years older than he was.

He looked at Mary and smiled sadly, 'at last Mary. I am a rich man.' He looked into her face for the longest time and turned to the radio. 'You make all my wishes come true. Even when I don't know I have wished it.'

'I'd like to look in on Iris now Dan.' He nodded and started tuning into other stations. 'It works better at night for some reason' she said as she left him to it.

Iris was asleep so she went back and watched Dan looking for stations and testing the volume up and down. Mary got herself a coffee and sat opposite him. 'It runs on a twelve-volt Dan, there's a brand new one in it.' He nodded mutely. Then 'thank you Mary.'

Dan found a station with a beautiful melody playing, 'see Mary you have brought much beauty into my life. Green fields, a winding river and music.' The soft smile on his face touched everyone.

There was quite a crowd gathering at the radio, so Mary finished her coffee and left, she walked over to her horse. She felt a hand on her wrist and turned half expecting to find Jack. But it was Dan's face she looked into. 'Thank you, Mary. How do I thank you for all you have done for me? For us?'

'No need to thank me Dan, just enjoy it.' Mary gazed off into the paddock. 'Look Dan. See the wheat growing, there will be a good harvest this year by the looks.'

He nodded and smiled, 'Someday I will find a way to repay you Mary.'

'Just be here Dan. That is enough.' It was Mary's turn to be self-conscious, she swung up in the saddle as if she didn't trust herself. 'Things will work out for you Dan, you'll see. Send for me when you need me, bye now.'

Dan nodded and stepped back, comforted by her words. Mary had left an old rifle with him to use for the three shots signal. She'd also told him to use it for hunting if he wanted. 'There are a lot of wild pigs in the area Dan that need thinning out' she'd said handing him a box of bullets. Just like her, he'd thought, to give him something and make him feel like he was doing her a favour by taking it. God yes!

Dans scratched his head as he stared at the ground. He wasn't much with a rifle. But how hard could it be? He felt a surge of excitement course through him that was life giving. He watched the woman ride off; she'd done it again. He'd go hunting and see if he could get them some meat. Dan went to the kitchen and asked Noreen if it would be alright for him to leave camp for an hour or two.

'Why yes Dan, of course, I don't expect there will be much change. Iris has had her dose and is sleeping peacefully. '

'I'm gunna take the rifle Noreen and see if I can get a wild pig.'

'Oh, Dan some nice pork how wonderful would that be.' Noreen had her hands clasped in front of her.

'No pressure hay' Dan laughed softly. 'You can listen to the radio for a while if you like Noreen. Take the edge off when I come home without a pig.'

Noreen laughed quietly. 'Thank you, Dan, I would love to listen to some nice music for a few moments. That would be wonderful. I will turn it up a little so as Iris might hear it to.'

'Alright Noreen, I'm going up the river towards the east. I'll tie the dog up and if you need me just let him go, he'll find me, and I'll come straight back.'

The dog, Mary had given to the camp to watch over them and he did a mighty fine job of that. He never failed to bark if he heard something in the night. A couple of times Dan had to go and rescue hobos that the dog had bailed up.

But the dog had loved Dan right from the start and always followed him around.

'Alright Dan, you go have some fun. Oh, and even a rabbit would be lovely. The kids brought back a couple of ducks they got with that slingshot you made them.' Noreen turned to face him now a serious look on her face. 'You are a good man Dan, one of the best. We struck it lucky the day we met you and your wife, and we have not forgotten how you helped us.'

'Oh, Noreen! For an intelligent woman you talk bloody nonsense sometimes. But thanks for letting me off for a few hours.' Dan turned and hurried off, he had the rifle, a skinning knife, some rope and about twenty bullets.

Ben was down on the riverbank catching fish, he always came

home with plenty of them. He'd go that way and let him know what the shots were about. So, Dan with his rifle over his shoulder, left the compound.

On his way he asked Wally, who was looking over the fencing they'd put up last month to keep Marys' animals out, if he wanted to go with him. The grin that lit up the young man's face found its way onto Dan's face.

'You any good with a rifle Wally?'

'Never tried Dan. Can I hold it?'

'Thought you'd never ask; you can carry it.' Dan was rewarded with another wide grin.

After they left Ben, they headed off following the river. They'd gone about a half a mile when Wally spotted them. A drift of seven pigs, heads down rooting around in the grass. Dan lifted his rifle to his shoulder and took aim at a not quite full-grown sow. He got the head in his sight and squeezed the trigger just like Mary had shown him.

Dan couldn't believe how quick the pig hit the ground. Wally jumped up and down and let out a yell then ran to look. Dan got to his feet and followed a little more warily. He watched as Wally lifted his foot and placed it on the pig.

He turned to Dan, 'This is gunna taste real good Dan.'

Dan reached the pig and looked down at it. 'Don't suppose you know anything about skinning them, Wally?' Dan watched the other pigs run off.

'No mate, not a clue but old Maynard will know. He seems to know everything there is to know especially when it comes to survival. I guess on account of him being in the war Dan.'

'How do you know all this? I can't get boo out of him.'

'We got a bit close over the past two years. To be honest he found me doing something stupid I'd have got five years for. Well anyway he got me out of it and took me under his wing. He told me "Better to starve out here free than starve in prison." I never forgot it.' He laughed apologetically and with a shrug said 'then he taught me how to look after myself so to speak. But I've never done anything shady since I joined you lot Dan. We'd never bring trouble down on you.'

'Good to hear that, Wally. That's right you two travelled together,

I remember you telling me. Yeah, he's a hard worker alright and an intelligent one. He doesn't take part in discussions about things he just gets in and does it and everyone follows suit. And it always works. Well, if you can ask him, I'd be grateful.' Dan shook his head and went on, 'I've asked him various things in the past, but he don't like to be questioned. In fact, he doesn't much enjoy conversation. Well, my hat off to him for looking after you young Wally.'

Wally grinned at the praise for his mentor who he was very fond of and from a man he was equally fond of. 'I think we should gut it though.'

When the men had it gutted and trussed to a tree branch, they shouldered it and began the walk home. Dan was deep in thought going over that shot and how they would enjoy eating the pig which incidentally was head shot. He hadn't seen the dog until it was nearly on him. He froze.

Dan stopped and looked at Wally and Wally saw all he needed to see on the big man's face. They dropped the pig and Wally put his hand on Dan's shoulder. 'You go mate, I'll see this gets home. Go on mate go, and my heart is with ya.'

Dan put his hand over Wally's for a second and dropped it to his side. He looked towards home shaking his head he said, 'it's near enough a quarter mile home Wally.'

Wally whacked him on the shoulder, 'I'll be fine man. Go, see to it. I'm heart sorry mate.'

'I can run that distance easy I'll send someone back to help you.' Dan remembered he had to give the signal to Mary, he needed to see her. He pointed the rifle to the sky and let off three shots, waited a moment then two more. casting a painfilled look at Wally he set off at a run. Wally was shouldering the pig on his own.

Dan was a big man six two and he had long legs. They'd carry him home fast to say farewell to Iris. He didn't know how to feel, he was sorry Iris had gone if that was why the dog had arrived, he might have just got off the chain. But Dan didn't think so, he almost hoped she was gone, her suffering at an end. Then he and the boys could let time heal their hearts, could get used to her being gone. Was he a monster he asked himself over and over?

Dan reached the compound to the sound of women weeping and he knew it was true. He asked Ben to send someone back along the river to help Wally. He walked in and went to Iris. Someone, probably Noreen, had covered her with a sheet. Someone pulled the curtain across their bed area to give him privacy and Dan pulled the sheet back from Iris' face to say goodbye.

He picked her up into his arms and rocked her back and forth. From somewhere deep inside him, a place he didn't know he had, great sobs erupted. Dan cried and cried until he was done. His body ached from the grief that had hit him. All the things he did and those he didn't, plaguing his mind.

When he was cried out, he sat and thought about a conversation he'd had with her about a week before. He'd come in and found her dressed and sitting on the chair. He'd sat on the side of the bed, and she'd started to speak. He listened.

'Dan, I need to tell you how much I have loved you all these years. I never found it hard to forgive you for anything, you were so deserving. No listen dearest. I have watched you fall in love, and I hope...'

'Well, you can just stop it, she is someone else's. So, I finally got my just deserts. Listen Iris I have always....'

'Shut up Dan. You have always been the best husband a girl could ask for; you cannot force yourself to love someone Dan. If you could, you would have done it. I cannot bear to think of you on your own. I hope you find the happiness you so deserve one day. You are a young man, what twenty-nine. Look after our boys and please don't grieve for me. My time is near Dan, and I just wanted you to know how happy you have made me. Now you go and make yourself happy dearest. It is your turn. Don't let anything stand in your way. I love you with all my heart. Now I will say good night, Dan, could you just ask Noreen to come. And remember when you find someone who makes you happy, makes you breath different, grab it with both hands. Kiss me Dan and go and live life.'

A tear slid down Dan's face. Damn her he'd thought, just when he thought he couldn't feel any more wretched. He leaned forward, took her in his arms and kissed her. Then he stood up and walked away.

He'd taken a few steps when he turned and walked back to her and, going down on his knees in front of her and sliding his arms around her, he pulled her gently in to his embrace. Dan gave her the kiss he knew she wanted with all the love he could muster and when he ran short of that he topped up with a heartfelt sympathy. It was a long and lingering kiss, gentle yet passionate. When he pulled back, she was smiling. He smiled softly at her, 'I love you to Iris and it would have been enough....'

'Are you alright Dan?'

Dan was jolted back to the present, the God awful present. Shaken from the God awful past into the God awful present. He stood up, 'yes, I am Noreen. What do I feel now Noreen, heartache because she's gone or relief that her suffering is through?'

Noreen put her hand on his arm 'Both Dan. If you can manage that then you are a good and loving soul.'

Dan was sitting at the table holding a son in each arm when he heard Mary coming. He rose slowly and walked to the door and looked out. There on the back of the cart was a long box. It was covered with a tarp, but he knew what it was. Mary was getting down from the horse. Thank God she's here was all he could think as he walked out into the yard.

She turned towards him and stopped, 'am I right Dan' she asked hesitantly? When he nodded slowly, she came towards him and when her arms came out to him, he fell into them. He cried into her neck and his arms went round her and crushed her to him. 'Mary' he said over and over. She pulled back and he reluctantly let her go. 'She's gone Mary.'

'Dan I will just go and see Noreen okay. Are you alright?' He nodded. 'Alright I will come back Dan, I'm not going to leave you now.' She smiled and he was comforted, so comforted.

Dan followed Mary back and sat back down at the table where his two boys snuggled up under his arms. He sat quietly holding them and suddenly knew he would be all right.

'How did she go Noreen' Mary asked?

'She just didn't waken Mary. She died in her sleep; I didn't even know till I came over to check on her. Oh, Mary it's for the best.

Awful thing to say I know.'

'No Noreen you are absolutely right. Dan will see it one day. Have you told him any of this?"

'No Mary he just got back. Ran all the way back I'd say. Could you talk to him Mary, he listens to you. Take him away from here for a while, just while we see to her. Do you have the coffin?'

Mary nodded, 'who's here Noreen to get it off the back of the cart?'

'Ben and Maynard are here and Samuel and Mathew. I'm sure we can manage Mary. Just keep him away for an hour or more if possible. She's clean and all but we need to prepare her.'

'I don't know where to take him and don't know if he'd come with me Noreen.'

Noreen thought for a bit and then she said, 'tell him you would like to see the grave site, Mary. That way you could check and make sure it's all ready for the funeral.'

'Okay Noreen, I'll give it a try.' Mary walked to the table where Dan was sitting holding his boys. Mary looked into the sons faces and they just looked startled. They had known their mother was dying but still. Mary put her hand on Dan's shoulder and his head came round to look at her. She looked into his tear- stained face and smiled softly.

As gently as she could she said 'Dan, can we go for a walk do you think? Maybe talk a little.'

'Yes Mary' he said and started to rise. 'Where do you want to go Mary?'

'Can we go to the riverbank Dan?'

'Yes Mary. You boys wait...'

'No Dan, why don't we all go, the fresh air will do us good. We can take the dog and let him bring some fun to the boys. Just for a little while Dan, we all need it.'

'Yes Mary, that sounds perfect.' He looked at his boys and motioned with his hand 'come' he said softly. They sprang to their feet, their little faces eager as they looked up at Mary. Like everyone else they loved her.

Dan followed Mary out the door and as he walked away with her, he took a deep breath. 'Feels good Mary to be out of there. Thank you, you always know, don't you? How do you do that Mary?'

'I know you Dan. I remember when my father died, when I finally got outside and got back to normal, and it felt good. There's nothing wrong with that. I breathed easy just the same as you. Doesn't mean you didn't love them doesn't mean you won't miss them, just means you decided to go on living.'

'How did you get so wise so young, woman.'

Once clear of the buildings Dan said to the boys 'go on boys have a run with the dog. It's all right lads. Go on now.' Mary smiled at him it was a nice side of him. They'd be alright this little family of three and they'd have the love and support of all the other people as well.

The two boys grinned up at him, 'thanks dad' they said, and they were gone chasing after the dog.

'Can we go and see where you have chosen for Iris' she asked? Dan nodded. Veering away to the left they walked over the rise and down to the riverbank.

Dan stopped and breathed the air, 'you know I love it here Mary. I bloody love it. Thanks for everything you've done for me Mary. You've always been there for me I'll give you that.' He reached out and took her hand in his, 'can we walk Mary, and can we hold hands like it only mattered to us? Just this once please, just this once. Hold my hand while we walk.' Dan turned and walked on taking her with him. 'I always feel that you are holding my hand Mary in everything I do. I have learned a lot from you. First, I learned that I love the land and the river. Also, I learned what it is to love, that it is more a privilege than a right and once you love someone no one else will do. I have learned to farm and grow things and I learned that I love these things to. And I have Learned also that I love to build.'

Mary held his hand; she knew he needed to talk and be comforted. Dan was talking now, 'I'm gunna send the boys to school next year Mary. I don't want them to be like me, well at least not because they have no choice about it. One day this cursed, bloody depression will be over and the war that's coming to.

And when it is I'll know because I am a rich man with the best damn radio money can buy. I'm flabbergasted Mary. You amaze me.' Dan Laughed softly as he gazed into her eyes.

'I thought you'd like it, I'm glad you like it. And that is a lot to learn Dan. Some people don't learn all that in a whole lifetime.'

'Yeah, well they didn't have you Mary, to push them and guide them and smile when they fall flat on their face.' He squeezed her hand and chuckled deep in his throat.

Mary looked up at him in amazement. The years were falling off him and the sadness and the tiredness were peeling off him in sheets. He smiled down at her and her breath caught in her throat. His excitement was palpable, electric and a little unnerving. 'You challenge me Mary, you know?'

Shortly they were at the grave and Mary noted that it had been prepared properly. Even with boards and ropes, ready to lower the coffin in the ground. They stood looking at it for a while and Dan said softly, 'there it is Mary, all done to specifications. The mortician will be happy with it. I'm happy with it.'

'It's lovely Dan you picked a pretty place for her.' She looked up at him, 'You know Dan, she died in her sleep. Didn't make a sound, Noreen went to check on her and…. I'm '

Dan smiled softly, 'thank you Mary.' He heaved a great sigh, 'a weight off my back that is. We married because she was expecting, you know? I don't think I did her any favours Mary. You can't love somebody you don't. And to be honest Mary I have spent the last twelve or so years feeling bloody wretched about it every bloody day. The guilt is a heavy burden. I tried over and over to find solace in the arms of other women, but I would just feel worse, so much worse Mary.'

He turned and still holding Mary's hand he walked away a bit. He sat under a tree on a patch of grass pulling Mary down beside him. After staring at the river, for some time he turned to her, 'when do you think they'll have the funeral, Mary?'

Mary studied his face 'well we need to get the funeral director out here, so I guess when he is ready.' She held on to his hand.

'Will we have time to let Jack know?'

'Yes Dan. I'll go into the post office shortly and let him know. We can keep that in mind when we are deciding which day, you know, to give him time if he can make it at all Dan. I will go from there to the funeral parlour.'

'Thanks Mary. Do you know I would do anything for you Mary?' He smiled at her 'just so you know.' He nodded his head, 'would you kiss me, Mary? Just once. Just this once and love me while you do? Love me just for today I need it. I wouldn't ask else Mary. Just give me today and I'll die happy.' He stood up and pulled her up to stand in front of him. 'Mary?'

Mary looked into his face, bright with hope his eyes shining with pain and love and happiness, all at once. It was the conflict in his eyes that got to her, and she found she was nodding. When his lips came down gently on hers something inside Mary sprang to life, something she suspected she might never get back in its box. A need that would never be sated.

Her lips parted and his tongue entered her mouth, and he kissed her with a love that needed no top up. Their bodies seemed to melt together, his arms holding her firm. He caressed her and nuzzled her neck. Kissing her again harder and more urgent she felt her knees shake but he held her firm.

For a time, Dan stood and just held her to him. He could hear the boys somewhere down river. 'Thank you, Mary,' he whispered in her ear. 'Just so you know Mary, I love you. I know you are starting something with Jack, and I have taken a liberty here today that may have caused you to be uncomfortable. I'm sorry Mary, so sorry. But I do appreciate that you did it to comfort me. Thankyou.' He held her at arm's length studying her face, 'Also just so you know Mary, I will always be here for you, and I will never love another. It's you I love and always will be.'

'Dan I…. I don't know what to say. I don't feel that I belong to anyone Dan. No, not really. I don't know how I…. I'm not sure… '

He smiled faintly, 'You don't need to say anything you know. You don't need to tell me how you feel about me Mary, I've always known.'

'Oh God Dan.' Mary's lips still tingled but her face burned white hot.

He turned about still holding her hand 'I think we had best go back now, I know you were sent to get me out of the way, and you did an excellent job. And you have cheered me up and soothed me, Mary.' He turned towards her, slipping his arms easily around her waist he held her close, looking into her eyes. 'Two things woman, never be afraid of me and never be embarrassed with me. In my eyes you can do no wrong see.' He smiled and kissed her again. How he loved her. Her arms were around him and he was home.

He walked on with her holding her hand, 'Let's go down river a way and find the boys. They love that dog, you know; he was a God send. And that radio will be a comfort to me Mary, I can listen to it and be reminded of your love for me at the same time.' He smiled at her, 'I'll remember this day forever and cherish it, Mary. But I warn you, I will be praying for more of them to.'

Mary pulled him to a stop 'Dan, it's true that…. Well Oh, damn it, it's true.'

Dan smiled down at her and pulling her into his arms again he held her while she cried, and Mary's arms went round him once again. Mary cried and cried. She sobbed until she was tired out. She cried for Iris, she cried for herself but most of all she cried for Dan. Mary cried for a love that was beautiful yet doomed. When she was finished, she sniffed and looking up at Dan she said, 'I will always love you Dan, right now I'm mighty confused.'

Dan took his hanky from his pocket and wiped her face. 'I know' he said simply with a smile. Taking her hand, Dan walked with her slowly along the riverbank and talked to her of general things. Stopping suddenly and turning to face her he said excitedly, 'I didn't tell you Mary, I shot a pig today. Got it right in the head, Wally's bringing it home.'

'Wow Dan, is that what we will have for tea tomorrow night?'

'Yes Mary. Will you come?'

'Of course, I will be around Dan until you get through this.'

'Thank you, Mary. And afterwards to I hope, Oh yes Mary, forever and a day. Right?'

She nodded and smiled up at him. 'Forever and ever Dan.'

'Lovely Mary, lovely.'

When they reached the boys, he called them to come home. 'Ohh, dad! Just a little bit longer, please.'

'No, come now.'

They ran up to him and showed him a dead lizard. His face darkened a little, 'did you kill it Kane?'

The boy of eight years looked up and nodded his head.

'Are you going to eat it boy?'

Kane shook his head.

'Yes or no, say it' Dans voice was a little gruff.

'No dad, I'm I'm not.'

'Did it attack you?' When Kane stood staring up at his father his lip trembling Dan spoke, his voice a little louder. 'Well, did it?'

'No dad.'

'Then you had no right to kill it. You carry this creature that you have maliciously killed, home and bury it. Then you say a prayer for it, and you humbly ask for forgiveness. Then you come and get me, and I will inspect the grave.'

'I'm sorry dad.'

'It's alright lad we are in enough pain. Come now, let's go home.' He held the boy's hand as he walked. He took the lizard from the boy and put it in a hanky in his pocket.

Bryce, the younger boy came round and held Mary's hand. They'd gone just a few feet when Dan stopped and hoisted his oldest son on his shoulders. They walked for a little way and Dan put him down. Turning now to Mary he went down on his knees 'your turn my lady'.

'Oh no, no Dan I couldn't. Don't be silly. I'm too heavy'

Dan took her hand as the boys ran round them shouting encouragement to Mary. Dan said to her now, 'You are not too heavy, and you are not too tall. You are not too anything Mary you are just right. Always remember that.'

Mary sat herself gingerly on his shoulders and he got to his feet. 'Dan I'm too heavy. Oh...' she started to laugh. He gave a hoot and ran around in a circle the boys laughing and yelling.

'There you see not too heavy. You are just right Mary, just right. The man who steals your heart will forever earn my ire and my envy. But have no fear my dear lady I will conceal it forever within my bosom.'

'What' shouted Kane. 'What does that mean dad?'

'Some day boy, God willing, you will know.'

He didn't know it, but he had sealed his love for Mary and hers for him. Mary wondered about Jack.

Before they climbed the rise to the path home Dan put her down and took her hand and squeezed it gently. 'Oh Mary, thank you.' He let her go and got down so Bryce could climb on his shoulder. The boy at six years old was about the same height and weight as his brother, and almost the dead spit of his father.

He hugged his father's head and said 'I love you dad. We'll always have you won't we dad?'

'You bet son you bet. Can you see home yet?'

'Yes, I can dad, yes, I can. I can see home dad.'

Mary saw the tear slid down Dan's face, but he turned his head and smiled at her. 'Thanks Mary. Home.'

They walked a little way and Dan let Bryce down from his shoulders. 'Now see Bryce, you are too heavy.' He laughed and they all laughed with him.

When they were nearly home the boys ran off, he asked softly, 'Will you stay for a cupper, Mary?'

'Dan I should go and get to the post office it will shut in just over an hour. I'll come straight back, and we can sit and talk for a bit. Alright Dan?'

'Okay Mary and thanks for everything. You've made this business so much easier. Hurry back woman. I shall miss you.'

'Righto, I'll go to the funeral parlour and put him on notice as well and see the doctor for we will need a death certificate. See you soon and Dan. It brings me joy to do things for you.' She reached out and took his hand and squeezed it.

Mary walked to Lilly and climbed up on her back, she'd ride with no saddle. She swung the horse about and cantered off along the road to town. She looked over her shoulder, and he was watching her go. She raised her hand and spurred her horse on.

Well, this afternoon would take some sorting out. Maybe she was reading too much into it, maybe he just needed some comfort. She shook her head, that wasn't like Dan. And how did she know that?

Dan had some very mixed feelings about Mary talking to Jack and he hated himself for it. He watched her for a while and smiled at the fact that nobody seemed even to notice she always wore pants. He assumed it was because she alone looked after herself. People had too much respect for her to criticize her. That and she looked good in them. She wore them quite tight and long enough for her and she wore her shirts untucked. A thrill surged through him.

His mind was dragged back to the present when Noreen asked if it was alright to place the coffin, with Iris in it, on the stand on the veranda. And so, Iris was carted by Dan and Wally and Ben and Maynard and placed outside. Dan knew there were too many people living in close quarters already to add a body in a coffin to the mix.

'Do you want the lid left up for viewing Dan?'

'No Noreen, I don't. Thank you.' Dan figured everyone had been through enough and as he made these decisions, he could see that those present were relieved but trying not to show it.

He got himself a coffee and had just about finished when Bryce came in the door. 'Dad, Kane has buried the lizard and he's sitting out there bawling his head off.'

'Oh no. Just wait here Bryce. Where is he?' Bryce pointed towards the back of the house.

Dan walked to the back and found Kane sniffing and wiping his tears on his sleeve. Dan handed him his hanky which he took.

'What are your tears for Kane?'

'Mum! What do you think?'

'Of course, I am sorry boy. I don't know what to say to you. She's not in pain anymore. She's in heaven with the angels.'

'How do you know?'

'Someone as good as your mother? Of course, she's in heaven. Come on son let's go inside.'

'I didn't want to put the bloody lizard in a hole. I don't want to put mum in one either.'

'It's where we go when we die lad. It's tough I know but her soul is not going in the hole. Her soul is free. It is free. Come on lad. Did you see the pig I got?'

'Did you shoot it dad? Oh, wow dad.' He looked Dan in the eye.

'We are going to eat it you, see? For tea tomorrow night.'

'Will you teach me to shoot one day dad?"

'Yes, lad I will.'

'Can we stay here forever dad?"

'Yes Kane. What do you think of your old dad as a farmer?'

'I think its great dad. Are you gunna marry Mary? I saw you holding her hand at the river.'

'Your mums not in the ground Kane. Do you plan to marry everyone who you hold their hand?'

'Yes, I only held Suzie's hand and I'm gunna marry her.'

'You held my hand today. Come on mate, let's go in.'

'Dad, it's like mum's been gone a long time.' The boy hung his head and whinged.

Dan picked him up and carried him a bit. 'You did a nice job burying that lizard lad. I'm proud of you, you had a job to do, and you were man enough to do it.' He hugged the boy and setting him down again he looked into the boy's face. 'I'm going to send you and your brother to school next year. And any of the other kids who want to go.'

'Oh dad, that's great. Bryce to, I'm glad!'

'Yep.' Dan took his hand, 'we'll have a tree this Christmas to. How about that?' Kane grinned up at his father, 'I like Mary dad.'

'Me to son, me to.' Dan smiled down on his son who was more like his mother. 'Maybe we'll have a feast to, and let Santa know where we are hay?'

Kane sighed but smiled up at his father 'yes dad. That's what we'll tell the little kids.' Dan chuckled and so did Kane.

Chapter 7

The day of the funeral was a grey day in September and everyone from the community was there and quite a few townsfolk as well. The blokes and a couple of the women who worked in town had got to know people. And they had been excellent ambassadors for the homeless in that community. At last, they had been accepted though the way had been hard. Dan didn't doubt that Mary had been their biggest advocate.

All the people in the community were decked out in their best, maybe a little ragged here and there but clean and neat. All shoes were shined checked by Dan himself. Even the children were clean and tidy and on their best behaviour. Dan was proud of his family, all of them.

When they lowered the coffin into the ground Dan stepped up and taking his tie off, he threw it in on top of it and wiped his eye. His sons who had been given ties for the occasion did the same. There wasn't a dry eye at the gravesite. Dan was very proud of his sons, he'd have to replace the borrowed ties.

Dan stood apart on his own with his boys while the priest said a few words. He stood opposite Mary and Jack. Dan had given up on trying to remain neutral, he was sick of listening to what a big man Jack is now. He'd like to throw Jack in the bloody river, but he also knew this was no time for conflict. Dan wanted Mary with a passion that frightened even him. Jack had Mary yet he ignored her so much of the time. Dan and most everyone else could see it hurt her.

Dan had spent the last few days trying to be nice to him, trying to overlook his shortcomings even make excuses for him. But Jack, he thought now was a braggart plain and simple. He thanked God the man would be leaving tomorrow. Well anyway he'd go along and wave goodbye to him and then he'd cuddle his girlfriend as he disappeared down the track. No Dan wouldn't be ignoring such a woman. Grab hold, with both hands is what she had said and both hands it would be. Dan knew in his heart there would be no denying his feelings for Mary.

Soon it was time to go back to the long house for some eats. Dan could see some doubt on the faces of the townsfolk, but they couldn't very well refuse really. Anyway, their curiosity drove them on inside. The women under Noreen's supervision had scrubbed and polished the place from top to bottom. Not that the place wasn't always clean and tidy and warm. Dan loved the ambience of the place and was certain everybody else did. They had all survived the harsh winter in good health. Even the babies.

Curtains were pulled across the sleeping areas and all bedding and clothing and curtains had been washed with hot water and soap, the place even smelled nice. They had done him proud. They had done themselves proud and they had done Mary proud. And above all they had done Iris proud. Her funeral was second to none as far as Dan was concerned.

He noted also the surprise that registered on their faces at the cleanliness and the nice ambiance of the home. The long table was polished and shining, with fisher's wax, and laden with good food presented on clean wooden platters, made by the men, simple but nice. Every inch of wood had been polished. The stools were pulled to the side so people could stand or sit.

People were surprised when the white sheet was pulled back and the buffet on the table was equal to anything they could provide in some cases better. The back legs of the pig had been roasted and sliced cold and the front leg of the pig had been cut into smaller pieces, soaked in brine and smoked because it had to be done in just over a week. It was sliced thinly in preparation for this occasion. Most of the chops were cooked and served cold on platters on a bed of cabbage leaves along with smoked and baked fish and rabbit.

Platters of pickled onions and cheeses supplied by Mary were a favourite. Small potatoes boiled and served with sliced onion and carrots. Beans and peas were served cold in bowls. Beetroot and steamed cold cauliflower looked good side by side on a big platter. Dried apricots were served up with damper jam and cream. And then there were the cakes the women had baked and though they weren't iced they were glazed. Also on the table were small bowls of cut up fruit, donated by Mary. In the centre of the table a floral arrangement made by the older children and smaller ones made by the younger children placed around the table. Everyone had contributed. Homemade lemonade was the only drink served.

In turn the townspeople, as they were introduced to Dan, were indeed impressed by the manner of the man. And they did note the respect even reverence that was paid to the man by his people, and the loving way they handled him in his grief. The men found him to be equal to any in the town and they liked him. They'd all heard how the man ran the camp and he did it with care and compassion and apparently, never a raised voice.

And if these people treated the big man with a reverence, Mary was a goddess to them. The towns people had been sceptical, and some had told her so. But she had just smiled at them.

Most of the people were taken with the older men who were cleaner, healthier, more alert, and slightly better kempt than any in town or anywhere including those in homes. They appeared to be sharp and happy. Someone remarked about this to Samuel and Ben. Ben had smiled and said softly 'it is because we are still useful. We bring in food for us and we help maintain our compound in a clean and orderly fashion. We tend to the gardens along with the other men. And we build.'

Samuel piped up, 'and we oversee playing and caring for our children, we teach them games. We, along with some of the others, are even teaching them to read and write, manners and reading and arithmetic for when we send them to school. Maynard here teaches them games and hunting and he is largely responsible for these lovely wooden plates we are eating from. Of course, he teaches carpentry and woodwork. Dan teaches them geography, history, farming honesty and love and tries to keep them abreast of current news. Ben here teaches them about building, how they go up and how they come down. Noreen, with Mary's help, teaches them about medicine, health, and hygiene. The other ladies teach them cooking and sewing and the like. Yes, even the boys.' He smiled, proud of himself and his home.

Most of the people had noted the radio these people had, and Dan had smiled inwardly. If he could just have five minutes alone with Mary. Bloody Jack was always hovering.

The children were very well mannered clean and well spoken. One of the blokes at the funeral was a schoolteacher, two of the girls cleaned at the school once a week so when he heard of the funeral, he had wanted to come and pay his respects and maybe take a look.

He was intrigued and stood talking to Ben and Dan and the others for a while. He asked to meet the children and again he was impressed by their manners and their attitude overall.

He looked at Dan and said, 'when you bring them to school come and see me, I am Josh Vance. I can help with getting them sorted into the grades best suited to their level of learning.' He leaned closer to Dan dropping his voice, 'May I congratulate you and yours on the excellent tutorage of your children, they are a credit to you sir. They are well informed, well-mannered, and bright. Yes indeed.'

Dan smiled at the man his heart full of the pride showing on his face. 'Thank you, Josh, I will look for you. We don't know how many of them yet probably all of them. About ten I think are school age.'

'A welcome boost to our school, I look forward to it.' Dan smiled at the man, he liked this Josh. He shook hands with the schoolteacher and went to see Mary.

He looked into Mary's face and smiled 'alright Mary?' Her face brightened and she smiled 'yes Dan. I'm fine actually.'

'That's good Mary.'

All too soon it was time to go. As the townspeople filed out passed Dan, they shook hands with him and offered their condolences once again. They felt they had stood in the presence of a shepherd with his flock. Dan spoke softly so as people strained to hear as he thanked them for coming. 'If we can ever be of assistance to the town, please let us know.'

There were a couple of young blokes from town talking to Jack and eyeing off the girls. Dan kept his calm though listening to Jack extolling his importance to the community, the country and the whole damn world in general was irking him. Then Jack went too far as he leaned over and made some rude remark about Melbourne girls.

Dan put his cup down gently on the table and went to stand close to Jack. The blokes walked away a bit.

Dan kept his voice low. 'What the hell do you think you're doing Jack? This is Iris' wake so if you can't be a bit more respectful clear off. Oh, and Jack, don't leave this compound until I have had a chance to speak to you.'

Equally as low Jack spat, 'always the big shot Dan.'

The people were all gone, and it had gotten dark. Dan was sitting alone out the front on the logs, and everyone thought to give him a minute. Mary had just finished helping clean up and unable to spot Jack anywhere she said goodbye to everyone. 'Thanks, Mary, for all you've done for us. Will we see you tomorrow, where's Jack? Oh well Dan will see you home love.' Everyone had noticed the change in Jack and how disrespectful he'd become.

Mary smiled, she was relieved Jack was missing and was eager to get going before he came back in. She walked outside and her breath caught in her throat. Dan sat alone and still had his suit on. He was more handsome than anyone she'd ever seen. No, she didn't want him to see her home either. She walked over to him.

He looked up and smiled, 'hello Mary, you off now?' She nodded and he said softly, 'where's Jack?'

'I don't know. I thought I 'd get going Dan.'

'Okay' he said standing up.

'I'll be alright Dan thanks. You must be tired.'

'Yeah, most likely Mary. Come on I'll take you home. What kind of man would I be?' He looked at her and raised his arms to the side, 'oh come on Mary, I'm wearing a suit.'

She had to laugh. They walked off and Mary whistled Lilly and Jim. The animals had been a big hit today, even the towns people made a fuss of them thought Mary as she thought back over the success of the day. She was glad these people were accepted. It was dark and Mary was glad Dan was there. 'You certainly gave Iris a wonderful send-off Dan. You did her proud.'

'Come on Mary, I've done nobody proud, and you know it.' His voice was gruff, and Mary kept silent.

He reached for her hand and taking it, he said softly 'sorry Mary. You know I'm sorry, don't you?'

She clasped his hand and said just as softly, 'yes Dan, I do,'

'Good girl. You are my good girl Mary and my bad girl. All in one.' He looked down at her and laughed softly. 'You won't go changing on me will you Mary?'

'Well anyway, I want to talk to you tomorrow, Dan.'

'What about woman.'

'Well then I would be talking to you tonight Dan and clearly I said I wish to talk to you tomorrow.'

'Ooh Mary. You are a bit feisty this evening, I must admit I do like it. Did you see those people today Mary admiring the radio? Yes, they were Mary. And their faces when they realised, we do not live in a filthy hovel. Tell me Mary, were any of council man James' men there?' He smiled and squeezed her hand tenderly. She shook her head, and he went on in a serious note, 'What do you suppose has got into Jack Mary?'

'He's behaving like a thug Dan. I noticed it more so today.'

'Okay Mary, I want to talk to you tomorrow to. After we put Jack on the train. Will you be all right here on your own tonight, Mary? If he comes around let off three shots and I shall come, running. Yes Mary, I will come running.' He stopped and looked into her face earnestly, 'unless you want him here Mary?'

Mary stared at him for a moment and said, 'let's just say I'm tired and I want to get off to bed.'

'Do you want me to stay Mary?'

'Please Dan, it is difficult to refuse you.'

'Okay Mary.' He walked on still holding her hand. After a while he said softly, 'I could sleep on the floor Mary, just so as I'd know you were safe.'

'What do you want to talk to me about Dan?'

'Well, there are a number of things Mary, but I think we need to have a conversation about the reaping next month.'

'Yes, we do Dan. But the reaping will probably be the next month. Mid to late November I think. We were a little late in.'

They got to Mary's house to see a light on inside. Dan stopped and told Mary to wait, and he'd go and see who it was.

'Well, isn't this cosey?' Jack stepped out of the shadows.

'I was just walking her home.' Dan cursed himself silently, he didn't owe this little thug any explanations.

'You have to hold her hand to walk her home?'

'Mind your own business, Jack. Go on inside Mary, I'll see you tomorrow.'

'Oh, so you do what he tells you to now. Well, you've been busy Dan while I'm away... '

'Just shut the hell up Jack. If I have to hear about how, you are out single handedly saving the world again, I'll pewk. Mary, go on inside woman like I asked. Please.'

A thoroughly unpleasant sneer made its way across Jacks face. 'When I left here a couple of months ago, she was my woman.'

'Oh, grow the hell up Jack. Mary is nobody's woman. Come on Jack let's go home.'

'I'm staying here I want to talk to her' Jack was very aggressive.

Mary stepped back; she was becoming frightened. 'Please Jack just go. I'll see you off tomorrow.'

Jack swung round to glare at her now. 'So, is he warming your bed now? You turned out to be a loose piece M......'

Jack got no farther as Dan punched him in the mouth and he staggered backwards. 'I heard some of the shit you were talking at the wake Jack. About the girls you've been bedding in Melbourne....'

Dan stopped talking Jack was coming at him. Dan took his coat off and stood waiting he checked on Mary and then kept his eyes on Jack who was lifting his fists.

'Alright! Alright then big man Dan. Come on have a go at me man. I'll knock your block off and then you can piss off home. And I'll stay here with my bloody woman. Come on.'

'Alright Jack but you'll get blood all down your shiny new uniform. And none of it will be mine.'

Mary stood back and watched as the two men rushed at each other. Dan struck Jack on the jaw and the blow knocked him senseless to the ground. He stood back and let Jack get up.

When the fight was over Jack staggered to his feet and yelled at Mary, 'I don't want you no more. You're welcome to her' he directed at Dan and ran off into the night. His parting shot over his shoulder 'I'm going back to the girls in Melbourne. They know what's what.'

Dan swung around and Mary was doubled up with her hands on her stomach. Dan took her gently in his arms and carried her inside. 'What is it love? Oh, Mary me darling what is wrong? Are you hurt Mary?'

Mary's face was ashen, and Dan took her inside and lay her gently on the bed. He sat on the side of the bed and held her hand. It was cold and shaking and he took her hands and rubbed them between his own. When she was calmed, he looked into her face, his eyes dark with concern.

'Talk to me Mary. Please.'

Mary put her head down, 'I can't Dan. I can't. I wish I could, but I just can't.

Please just leave me '

'Mary, have you forgotten so quickly? I told you to never be afraid of me and never be embarrassed.' He put his hand under her chin and lifted her face to look at him. His face was full of love and adoration. Mary was surprised to see he was a little amused.

He went on softly, 'Mary… I told you to go into the house when I realised there was no avoiding a fight. You took no notice of me Mary and you could have lost the baby,' He smiled softly.

'Oh Dan. Oh my God Dan. I am so…. How….?'

'Hush now woman' he said slipping his arms around her. He held her and waited for her to stop crying. Then he lay himself gently down beside her and took the woman in both arms and held her. Held her gently and in the darkness of the bedroom he kissed her. And they both knew their fates lay in each other.

Dan lay there like that until Mary was sleeping peacefully and then he went to the kitchen and sat before the fire. He wasn't going to leave that woman here on her own tonight. He'd waken her just before first light and then he'd go.

Mary came to just before the dawn and went out to the kitchen, Dan had gone home. She found herself wishing he'd stayed. At the doorway she stopped abruptly and stared at the man with the dark hair and still in a dark suit sprawled in a chair asleep. She walked over to him and nudged him awake. His hands reached for her pulling her down on his knee. He found her responsive warm and soft in his arms.

'God Mary, I love you.' His voice was sleepy, and it sent a thrill down her spine. He drew a deep breath and held her. Shifting her off his knee he said now, 'I best be going Mary. It'll be daylight soon.' He stood up.

'So, you just going to sneak off Dan. Without so much as a kiss goodbye.'

'Nay, never woman. Never.' He kissed her long and tender. He walked to the door and turned, 'now Mary, you stay here and rest. I'll come back this afternoon after I've put Jack on the train. I don't really want you to come Mary, not after last night.' He walked back and took her in his arms, 'I think you are having a girl' he laughed softly, 'a little daughter my love. Think on it. How wonderful you are Mary.' His face turned serious, 'I will stand by you, woman just like you've always stood by me. And you hold your head up now, you've done nothing wrong. Hear me?' He smiled, kissed her gently and left.

Out on the road his heart sang, he would marry that girl one day. When the baby was here, and she was a bit older. Though he knew the baby was Jack's, he wouldn't be telling him. Mary hadn't told him so that was telling.

Dan was almost home when the first light tinged the sky in the east. God, he hoped Jack was gone. He didn't feel like coming face to face with him, but he knew he must. As if on cue Jack materialised out of the gloom.

'So, you are sleeping with her Dan?' He threw his hands up and said 'I'm not trying to start anything Dan. Honest. Those girls I talked about. Well, it's just one girl and I slept with her just once and she's pregnant Dan. How do you like that for luck? I don't know Dan;

I was just lonely and she… well she was very convincing.'

'Well now I have a question for you. Did you sleep with Mary this trip?"

'I tried to Dan, but she wouldn't have me.'

'Shit, you're a piece of work Jack. Well, she's not coming to the station. Don't tell anyone this', he indicated Jack's face, 'had anything to do with Mary.'

'No, I wouldn't Dan. I'm sorry. I'm so sorry Dan. I'll never cause Mary or you any more trouble. I promise. Now get in and get out of your suit Dan. Was she alright when you left her? You're a good man you know?'

'She was fine Jack, just fine.' Dan went to walk off but stopped, 'Jack, you must have slept with that girl as soon as you got to Melbourne. Lonely my arse Jack.' Dan's face softened now, 'she doesn't want you no more Jack anyway. Mary that is.'

'She always liked you better Dan. No hard feelings, you're the better man. I guess I always knew when Iris died, I'd have my work cut out keeping her. Knew you'd come for her.'

Dan's face softened, 'Jack, think before you jump in to marrying this woman and consider the possibility she's lying about the baby and if she is pregnant, that you are most likely not the bloody father. I did that and my last ten years were miserable. And Iris deserved somebody who loved her. Just think on it for Christ's sake. And next time you come home leave your newfound ego in Melbourne hay. For Christ's sake man.'

'Yes, Dan I will. Does that mean I can come home again one day?'

'Yes Jack. You get us a coffee and I'll turn into a pumpkin.'

'A what Dan?'

'Oh, never mind Jack, come on.'

When Dan put Jack on the train, he felt a sense of loss. Things would never be the same between them that is if he ever did come back. Dan put his feelings aside and hugged Jack at the station. These were uncertain times. People starving all over and war on the horizon.

Some didn't believe that war would come but Dan knew it in his heart. He hoped it would be over soon and that he wouldn't have to send his sons. Dan himself was only twenty-nine and he knew if things got desperate, they'd call on him.

His mind went to Mary as he trudged along with everyone else. He'd get across there to see her as soon as they got back. He hoped she was alright, her and the baby. A smile made its way into his heart, a smile the like of which he'd never experienced. Suddenly he needed to get to Mary and make sure she was alright.

He looked around at the faces of his people, his family. Sadness registered on most of their faces. Some of them had realised that Jack's behaviour was probably fear. The children still idolised him and the older men had some idea what was in front of Jack. They knew how it felt.

Bryce sidled up to his father and sensing what was in the big man's heart he took his hand. 'Are you really gunna send us kids to school dad?'

Dan smiled down at the boy who was big for his age, 'yes son. You wanna go?'

'Hell yeah' Bryce had a grin on his face now.

'You know you can't use that language at school. You'll get told to go and stand in the corridor. And I am not paying good money for you to get familiar with the damn corridor.' He smiled down at his son.

Bryce threw his head back and laughed. 'You never know dad; I might want to be a painter.'

They both laughed, it felt good. Dan hadn't heard the boy laugh since they'd buried his mother. School would be best for all these kids.

Chapter 8

*W*hen Dan walked into Mary's shanty she was nowhere to be seen. He panicked. 'Mary' he bellowed. 'God woman where are you? Mary.'

'Well, you can't come over after the baby's born, not with all that racket Dan.'

Dan spun around and watched Mary walk in the door. 'I'm sorry woman I couldn't find you. Are you alright Mary?'

She nodded and smiled. 'I'll get us some tea. How was Jack?'

Dan sat down and said softly, 'he was alright Mary. It turns out he's got a girl in the city. He is fine about us Mary. Not that we are on together Mary, not that. But he knows how I feel.'

Dan sat quietly as he watched the woman get them a cup of tea. He remained quiet when she sat down, waiting for her to say what she had to say. 'Does he know how I feel Dan?'

'Do you?'

Mary smiled. 'Anyway Dan, I wanted to talk to you.'

'Yes, I know Mary. Please go ahead.'

'Well, it's just this. I have grown up amongst wheat crops Dan and that crop you sewed is amongst the best I've ever seen. Now aside from the acres we use for housing and animals and gardens, we could plant wheat in all the rest. It would yield well over four thousand bushels. Dan if we planted the lot, the whole eighty acres or so, we could make well over a thousand pounds a year, probably closer to two thousand. Think on it, Dan. We'd still have our acreage for gardening and such.'

An excitement was making itself felt in Dans belly the like of which most men don't dare dream. 'We'd need another four Lilly's but....'

'Well Dan, I was thinking more of buying a tractor with plough and seeder.

Glenn next door is selling one. It's a good one Dan only a few years old and it has a harvester as well. Think on that.'

'How could we afford it Mary? Wouldn't it cost a fortune?'

'Yes Dan, he wants two hundred and fifty pounds for the plant. I have that, Dan; dad had a lot of money saved and his father before him and I have saved as well. We could get a truck to, just a small one to cart the hay. Just think about it Dan. Berty Hemlock has a truck in his yard he wants one hundred pounds for. It is only two years old.'

Dan took a swig from his cup and put it down, he was thinking about it alright. His head was swimming with it. He said thoughtfully, 'have you made your mind up about this Mary? You are having a baby next year....'

'Yes, but I have you Dan, you and I could do it. We'd split the money Dan. What do you say? Think what you could do with that kind of money Dan.' Dan looked thoughtful then 'what's brought this on Mary?'

'Well, we need a harvester for the wheat we have in so I thought instead of borrowing or hiring one we could buy one. Then I saw that notice about Glenn next door. Well?'

Dan smiled and Mary could see the light in his eyes. He was saying now 'I don't mean to be rude Mary, but will all this leave you broke?'

Mary smiled and said 'no not really Dan. But we'd have the tractor and harvester and so if the first year and even the second year are bad, we could just try again. And if the worst comes to the worst, we sell the lot and go back to market garden. Except that we would go in for it in a big way.' Mary looked at Dan and smiled 'and buy another two Lilly's. We'd have the truck to cart the vegies to market, we could take them farther afield and do maybe three or four markets a month. The world is gunna need food Dan and the horse and cart are well and truly out of date. As much as I love them, they are Dan.'

'Alright Mary. When are you going to have a look at the tractor?'

'Well, I'm going over there to get it tomorrow Dan and I was hoping to kill two birds with one stone. He is selling young lambs just off their mother. It's a bit early but we could get a few of them tomorrow to.'

'Lambs Mary?'

'Yes Dan, you get a few lambs to eat the stubble left in the paddock before it's time to seed again. Well, then you eat them.' Mary smiled at him. 'You are such a city slicker Dan.'

'Is that right woman' he smiled as he got to his feet. He pulled her to her feet and held her to him, 'will you be careful tomorrow baby?'

'What are you talking about? You are coming with me; we do this together or not at all. And didn't you used to drive a truck?'

Dan's face was aglow, 'yes I did.'

'Well, you can drive the tractor home and pull the header behind it. Lilly will pull the cart home with the seeder equipment and the lambs and such.' Mary looked thoughtful, 'then next week if we are successful, you can drive the truck home. Oh, you do come in handy Dan.'

Dan laughed and hugged her to him. 'Are you sure Mary, we could probably manage just getting another horse....'

'No Dan, like you said I will be good and pregnant next year, and I won't be able to help you. It would take two of us. We need to do it this way. And with so many of your men out working an....'

'When are you due Mary?'

'I think in March. Right when we'd need to be getting started. Do you think you can handle it Dan, I know you can, but do you want to?'

'Of course, I can Mary and thank you from the bottom of my heart for including me although why me?' She looked at him quizzically so he went on, 'Well okay Mary, I can be back here at first light.'

'I'll pick you up. Glenn's property is across the highway so I will need to use the gate down near you.' Mary lifted her hand and pushed some dark hair back from his forehead.

Dan dropped his head and kissed her. Falling to his knees he held her belly to him. 'On closer inspection Mary…. You are starting to show. Yes, Mary you are.'

She smiled down at him and bent forward to kiss the top of his head. 'Are you more excited about the baby than the whole tractor thing.'

He stood up 'oh Mary, I am most excited about the tractor thing. I cannot believe we are going to do this. I just worry Mary.'

'We'll still have the gardens and the market Dan. We can still make money. Nothing will change except that we'll have about eighty acres of wheat instead of five. If all else fails, we will put in as many acres as we can with Lilly. And we'll go from there.' She pulled him up to his feet and took him in her arms, 'at the end of the day we'll still have each other and three kids instead of two.'

Dan's head swam. 'I have never used a tractor woman.'

'I have never had a baby.' She shrugged and smiled. 'I have another surprise for you.' Taking his hand, she led him from the house down to the river.

Dan stared down at the picnic she had made. 'We are celebrating Mary. Mary when are we going to tell people about the baby?'

She hugged him again 'soon. You are very beautiful Dan.'

'Oh, Jesus' woman, the things you say.' He sat down on the blanket and pulled her down beside him and took her in his arms.

'The food Dan. I spent too long making it to just let it spoil.'

'Just a moment Mary.' He kissed her. 'I am most excited about the baby Mary, and I love that you have said we will have three children. Yes, I'll put my back to the plough woman, and I'll put it to anything else you might want.'

Dan lay down with Mary on the bank of the Murrumbidgee and held her to him. The birds sang high in the trees and Dans heart righted itself there in the shade of the big river gum. He didn't quite know how to feel but he knew he loved this woman. A kookaburra laughed heartily, and Dan smiled lazily pulling Mary closer.

After he'd eaten and satisfied himself that Mary was okay, he told her he had to go home to the boys for a bit. 'I have some jobs to do around about.'

'Alright Dan, I'll pick you up at breakfast time, so get some rest tonight.'

'Yes Mary, I will drive your tractor home in the morrow, and I do look forward to it.' He took her in his arms and kissed her tenderly on the lips. 'Don't forget Mary, three shots if you need help and two shots if you need me.' He helped her carry the picnic remains into the hut and as he turned to leave, he said 'if you need me Mary, two shots. For any reason' he winked.

'Go on with you, you are a constant temptation Dan.'

'That's good to hear woman. Tomorrow then, bright and early.'

Dan couldn't sleep, he had an excitement in the pit of his belly that was such that he thought he would burst. He'd keep it all to himself and see how things turned out tomorrow. He tossed and turned for a while then sat up and went to get a cup of tea.

Mary was on his mind, he was finding it hard to wait for her, but wait he must. He knew she loved him he could see it in her eyes, had done soon after they'd met. He felt just awful about being so damned happy with his wife just gone. It wasn't right.

'Feel like some company son?'

Dan looked up as Ben got himself a coffee. He smiled at the older man who always seemed to know when he did need some company. 'Just couldn't sleep Ben' he said quietly.

Ben sat down and smiled at Dan, he'd always liked the man, felt better when he was around. Ben was well aware they all pretty much felt that way. 'You've had a huge week Dan. I'd have been surprised if you didn't have a few sleepless nights. You wanna talk about it, son?'

'Well, I do but I just don't know how things are going to turn out Ben. So much is changing, I don't know how to feel. I guess the thing that's really getting to me is the guilt, Ben. I am glad she is gone, glad she's out of it. Out of that damn bed.' Dan lowered his head; he could feel the hot tears threatening to spill over. He had to hold them back.

Ben reached across the table and put his hand on Dan's. That simple act of kindness and love brought him undone. He cried quietly until he thought it would kill him. Ben wished there were something he could say but he knew there wasn't. Soon enough Dan was cried out and he took out his hanky and wiped his face. 'Sorry Ben, dunno where that bloody came from.' He blew his nose and put his hanky in his pocket.

'I do son. Your heart is being torn in all different ways. Just remember that you will get past this, and life will be good again. You have a lot to look forward to. I'm glad you let it out though son, no good bottling it all up.' He looked directly into the big man's eyes now, 'Mary has been a big help to you Dan. You were lucky to have her.'

Dan stared into the face of the older man and knew it would do no good to try and deny anything. He dropped his eyes and nodded his head. 'Very lucky indeed Ben.' He squirmed in his seat for a while and Ben tried to keep a straight face. Finally, Dan spoke in a soft voice 'okay Ben, what's the talk?'

To Dan's surprise the old man laughed softly, 'You can't keep anything a secret Dan. Not you.'

Dan smiled across at the old man and spoke softly, 'you didn't get it right there Ben. I was lucky to have all of you.'

Ben looked down at the table and raised his eyebrows, 'and Mary is lucky that son of a bitch high tailed it back to Melbourne. She is also lucky to have you. We are all lucky to have you.' He took a deep breath and ploughed on, 'all these years Dan, you looked after your wife. You remained faithful, loyal, and steadfast. I have never known you to be anything but kind both to her and your children and in fact all of us. Now you deserve some happiness son and not a person here would say otherwise. No son, the talk is we are bloody thrilled.' The old man swallowed a few times and keeping his eyes down he said softly, 'Iris was thrilled to Dan.'

Ben finished his coffee and got up from the table. He put his hand on Dan's shoulder and said 'goodnight son. Get some sleep if you can manage it.'

When next Dan climbed into his bed he slept like a baby. He had a big day tomorrow, an awfully big day. A new life, one that he would embrace. With both hands.

Mary got on the way to the long house just after sunrise. She had done some tossing and turning of her own. She had a powerful need in her for a certain tall dark-haired man but didn't know what she should or shouldn't do about it.

In the end she had decided to just get on with it and let things happen naturally. Not only was Dan's wife not long in the ground but she, herself was pregnant to another man. She tried not to think about it. Dan was right she would be showing soon, and she would like to tell people before they guessed. But not just yet, she wasn't too far along, and she wasn't showing very much. She smiled to herself as she remembered his excitement.

As she approached the gate, she was not surprised to see Dan lounging against it waiting for her. Everything seemed so simple when she was with him, he made everything seem normal even wonderful. Even the fact that she was expecting a baby out of wedlock. She pulled up and Dan shut the gate and climbed up and sat beside her. He'd told Ben that he was going to look at some farming equipment Mary wanted to buy.

'Morning Mary me darling. How was your night?'

'Good thanks. I was too excited to sleep much though' she grinned.

'Me to Mary, me to. I can't ever remember being this excited about anything. Except you Mary, you will always be the exception.'

'I know Dan.' She looked at him now, 'I think we are doing the right thing though; Greg looks after his equipment. Dad always said that about him to.'

Dan nodded and leaning across, kissed her on the cheek. She turned her head, and he kissed her, 'how are you feeling this morning' he said patting her stomach?

'Better now Dan, much better.' They talked as they plodded along the road.

———∿∿∘℮☞◎☜∘◦∿∿———

It was on the way home that it hit Dan, the enormity of it. He was going to be a farmer with the woman he loved and raise two sons and a daughter. Life just didn't get any better. He'd got the hang of the tractor though he couldn't go very fast. Neither could Mary who had to pull heavy equipment with Lilly. It felt good to be behind the wheel again.

He looked over his shoulder to check if Mary was alright. Dan didn't know how he was going to manage to wait for her, but he would take that a day at a time. He'd taken his wedding ring off last night and maybe that was why he'd cried. He'd always felt bad that the ring had never meant much to him. He'd worn it for Iris more than anything.

They arrived at the long house to the surprised stares of everyone. The noise of the tractor had brought them out to look and there was their Dan driving it.

Bryce had tears in his eyes and Dan felt bad he hadn't taken the kid. Kane was puffed up with pride for his father and grinning from ear to ear.

Dan brought the tractor to a stop just as Ben came up. 'So, this is the farm equipment Dan. Looks serious son. I think you are going to put in a bit more than five acres huh?' Ben was grinning from ear to ear.

Dan was grinning back at him as he turned the key and killed the motor. Noreen walked up to him smiling, 'What are you doing driving this monstrosity, Dan?'

The children and the older men were milling around him looking it over and Dan had to shoo them out of the way so he could get down. Wally was one of them and he said now 'you kept this quiet man, hope we are Gunna get a ride on it?'

Dan smiled and clapped him on the shoulder. 'You shall son, you surely shall.' He was rewarded with one of Wally's wide grins.

Mary pulled up with Lilly and the children were soon pulled away to her and the horse, ever their favourites. A UFO could land, and they'd look it over and go straight to Mary and Lilly.

Mary walked over to the tractor, and Noreen smiled at her 'the kettle is boiling you two, I suppose you could trash a cuppa.'

Mary smiled and nodded, as she walked towards the woman. Just at that moment the dog ran straight at her and jumped up for a pat putting his front paws on Mary's stomach. Dan rushed in and shooed the dog away gruffly and took Mary's arm and asked her if she was okay.

She nodded and he walked beside her shielding her now and Noreen looked Mary over with a practiced eye. She realised with a shock what Mary's condition was. I should have known she admonished herself. God, she'd have a word with Mary and let her know it was alright and that no one would judge her, no sir.

Mary turned and walked away with the woman, she saw the truth in the older woman's eyes and smiled at her. 'Thankyou Noreen. I will have need of you by and by.'

'I'll be here love and I won't be the only one. We'll talk soon hay?' Noreen couldn't help it and she pulled the child as she thought of her, into her arms.

Looking over Mary's head she looked into Dan's face and the gratitude on it was overwhelming. She did realise that it wasn't Dan's. Must be Jack's she thought despairingly. For this to happen to Mary of all people.

Ben had watched the exchange from the corner of his eye and smiled sadly to himself. So, the young mongrel had done this and then hightailed it out. He would like to get hold of him right now.

Ben also realised that that was probably why Dan was spending so much time with her. Not that he was blind to how Dan felt. He wondered if Dan would be willing to take her on. He thought he would, but still.

He observed the look on the big man's face as he watched her walk away and smiled. Most of the adults there realised the truth to and only concern showed up on their faces. Mary might be fallen but she was a fallen hero. A saviour, their damn saviour.

Dan flicked his eyes around the group and realised they would be spared the ordeal of making any big announcements. Wally was still non plussed, he'd need to be told. The children could wait, Mary had said she wanted to wait until, they were sure.

Ben strode over to Dan now. 'Am I right in what I assume son' he asked gently?

Dan looked into Ben's kindly face full of love and concern and nodded.

'Yes Ben.'

'So, the little mongrel didn't high tail it out quite soon enough. I'd like to get my hands on him. You know son I always thought young Jack was a decent sort of a bloke.'

Dan patted the older man on the shoulder now smiling gently. 'It'll all work out alright Ben, have no fear. She has us Ben.' He turned towards the tractor, 'what do you think Ben? No more walking along behind Lilly hay.'

'She served us well Dan. Speaking of which, we are gunna have to harvest potatoes and pumpkins soon, and maybe some cabbages.' Ben gazed at the tractor, the light burning just as brightly in his eyes as it was in Dan's. 'Come on inside son, get a cuppa and tell us all about it. The tractor that is.'

Dan sat with Mary, now that the truth was out it didn't matter if he was seen to be protective. Mary sat with the women after Dan had gone to speak with the men.

There was an uncomfortable silence and one of the younger women cleared her throat. 'Oh, come on can we talk about it?'

No one spoke and Mary realised it was up to her. 'Of course. If that's what everyone wants' she smiled.

Noreen sat forward in her chair saying gently, 'I always thought Jack was a nice man. But who knew he'd do this and then get some other girl in trouble as soon as he got to the city.' Noreen stopped talking at the look on Mary's face.

Mary sat opening and closing her mouth for a while then dropping her head and shaking it, in a mere whisper she said, 'Jack did not do this.' Everyone there thought they'd heard wrong and then Mary lifted her head and looked into Noreen's face. She said, 'Jack and I were never lovers Noreen.' She dropped her head again.

Noreen found her voice 'then who did Mary?' A bad feeling was finding its way into Noreen's stomach, the realisation almost stopping her breath. She was remembering that Mary had been bashed and burgled. She stared at the top of Mary's head. 'Mary?'

Mary looked up and looked beseechingly at Noreen. 'Please Noreen. I'd like to not speak of it ever again. Dan must never know.'

'But Mary, he thinks it was Jack.'

'Yes, I know he should be told. Well go on Noreen then tell him.' Mary had watched Dan go out the back with Wally and Ben.

She got up suddenly, 'I have to go Noreen, there are lambs on the cart. I have to get them home. Say goodbye to Dan and Ben and all. I'm sorry Noreen I don't know what to do.'

'No please Mary don't leave honey. You need help if you've been …., you know. Oh God Mary……'

Mary marched to the door and out into the yard. 'I will talk another day Noreen, I promise. You are right he should know.' The tears spilled over and ran down her cheeks. Noreen felt desperate.

Mary was nearly over at the cart and Noreen was holding her arm. 'Please Mary.'

Dan came round the corner and wondered what the hell had gone on. He went to hurry across to Mary, but she was up on the cart and gone.

'Mary' he called out, but she didn't look back. 'Mary!' Mary urged the horse on.

Dan swung round to Noreen, 'what is it, Noreen? What happened?' Noreen looked down and Dan took her arms gently and shaking them 'please Noreen, what is it?' He looked after the horse wondering if he could catch her and if he should try.

Noreen pulled on his arm now, 'Dan, we need to talk but just you and I. Come, sit with me on the log. By the time I tell you everyone will bloody know anyway.'

Dan sat in stunned silence as Noreen started to talk. 'We were all talking, and Mary's condition came up. Dan, we told Mary we were a bit surprised at Jacks behaviour. She told us that Jack was not responsible, that they had never been lovers. She didn't want to talk about it and didn't want you to know.'

'Jesus' woman, know what?' A memory, almost gone, flitted back across Dans vision. Mary coming late for work her face all puffed and swollen. Dan gave vent to a great sob. 'No ! No Noreen. Tell me I am wrong. Noreen!' Dan gave another great sob and another until he was sobbing. He himself had let her work all bloody day. All day that day she had worked. On the plough and on the shovel.

Noreen was relieved to see Ben running across to them, he fell to his knees in front of the big man he loved as a son. 'I'm sorry son… I'm….'

Wally who had heard all of it now came over and got Kane and Bryce. He took them away to let the grownups sort it out he told them and yes, their dad was fine. Wally's heart had broken.

Ben put his arms around Dan. Jesus he thought, who bloody saw this coming? Ben was thinking clearly and realised that Mary would be a bit farther along than a couple of months, maybe five? All this time. All this time the poor little bugger had kept it to herself, had asked for no help. But she had gone on helping all of them. Ben broke down and cried in Dan's arms.

When they were all cried out Noreen looked at Dan. 'Go to her Dan. Someone should be with her. She has carried this load on her own long enough. I messed up Dan, I'm sorry. Oh, Dan go to her.'

Dan looked at Noreen, 'I have no idea how to handle this, Noreen. I don't.'

'She will rather have you there Dan. That girl loves you; do you know that?'

Dan looked at Noreen through reddened eyes and nodded. Yes, he did. He didn't act like it, but he loved her to.

Noreen put her hand on his shoulder, 'be fair on yourself Dan, you didn't know.'

'Oh Noreen' he said looking down he turned to the tractor. 'I have to take that over there anyway.'

'Stay if she needs you Dan. Stay as long as you have to.'

Dan put his hand up and squeezed her hand, 'yes, I will Noreen. Yes, I will.'

When Dan arrived at Mary's place he walked into the house. The cart was empty, and the lambs were grazing in the yard and Lilly to. 'Mary' he called. 'Mary where are you?'

He walked from room to room calling her name. He felt a panic go through him as he realised, she was not there. He ran out of the house and down to the riverbank. He looked up and down and there was no sign of her. 'Mary' he called again looking about him. 'I'm not leaving Mary. Not till I see you.'

He waited a moment or two and then called again, 'I am here Mary. I'm here….

For the love of God woman, I need to see you. I need your forgiveness. Please!'

Dan sat under the tree where they'd had the picnic the day before. He cried again, softly. His heart was aching for the woman. But then she wasn't a woman she was a girl and she had been violated with no one to go to for help.

He threw his head back and screamed her name. 'Mary! I'm sorry.' And again 'I'm sorry.' But she never answered him. He lay down on the riverbank and waited. At intervals during the night, he called to her.

Around midnight Dan got to his feet, he would look to see if she had taken anything with her. He did realise he probably wouldn't be able to tell. God he was useless he told himself over and over again. It was early hours of the morning before Dan collapsed on the riverbank and fell asleep.

He never heard Mary walk past him and enter the house. Mary cleaned herself as best she could in the dark and, taking a blanket, she went to sleep farther down the river. She was sorry for Dan, but she just couldn't face him or anyone else. Not now. Mary made it around a bend before she too collapsed unconscious.

Dan woke with a start and looked about him. It was breaking day; he ran to the house to see if she was back. He slipped on something in the doorway and when he looked, he was horror-stricken. He had slipped in blood, a good deal of it.

He ran through the house and out into the yard. Something was wrong, he had to find her. He stood trying to make up his mind which way to go. A soft but urgent whiney from Lilly brought his head round and caused his heart to skip a beat. He ran towards the sound.

Rounding a tree and walking passed Lilly, he saw her. She was asleep and as white as a sheet; Jim had curled up beside her. On his knees now, Dan gently pulled her leg back towards him and the gasp he let out was half a sob.

Between her legs was a lot of blood and he knew what had happened. His little girl lay lifeless in Mary's lap under the blanket.

Coming to himself he slid his arms under her and lifted her up. He went to the hut he'd come back for the baby. He'd have to be quick about it too he told himself.

He placed Mary on the mat in front of the stove. Running back, he retrieved the tiny form, wrapped it in cloth and put it on a shelf in the veranda. Dan went to the kitchen and got a fire going and put the kettle on and went outside and let off three shots.

Returning to the kitchen he placed the spare mattress on the floor and covering it with a sheet and a couple of towels he put Mary gently on it. She was cold. Dan covered her with a blanket and did his best to clean her. He got a cup of tea for himself and one for her if she woke up.

A very breathless Wally ran in the door and stopped dead his heart in his mouth. 'Is she....?'

'She's sleeping Wally, can you sit here while I go and bring Noreen? She needs help.'

'Of course, Dan but hurry will you. Did....?'

'Yes Wally, she lost it.' Dan ran to the door saying as he did so 'I will be as quick as I can.'

He returned with Noreen on the tractor, he hadn't told her anything. He didn't have to. When Noreen saw Mary, she let out a sob and turned to the men.

'Can you leave us for a few moments please.'

Noreen examined Mary and knew that she would probably be alright. She saw that Dan had cleaned her, but Noreen knew it had to be done more thoroughly. When she was finished, she padded between her legs, covered her and called to Dan.

Dan came in the door and sat beside Mary on the floor. Noreen told him 'You did a good job Dan and putting her in front of the fire was good thinking. I think she'll be alright Dan. I will stay until she wakes up.' Noreen looked down at the sleeping girl, 'this would have been very painful.'

Mary woke up at around lunch time and smiled weakly at Noreen. 'I think I ....

I.... think....'

'I know love,' said Noreen. She stroked Mary's hair. 'Is Dan gone?'

'No love, he just went out for some fresh air.'

'Does he know?'

'Yes love. He found you and brought you home.'

Dan walked in the door and rushed to her. 'Mary, oh Mary thank God.'

Noreen got up and picked up her cup and left the two alone. She walked to the river bank her heart was breaking. She gave in to the tears and let them fall down her face. An awkward Wally put his arm about her.

Dan lay himself down beside Mary and took her in his arms. He held her for several minutes before she spoke. 'I'm sorry Dan.'

'Oh Mary, I'm the one who should be sorry.'

'I love you.'

He held her to him, 'I love you to woman.' They cried together there on the floor in each other's arms.

When they stopped Mary asked, 'do you have to go Dan?'

'No Mary I aint leaving you again. Not now and not ever. I mean it Mary and we'll get married as soon as possible.'

'You haven't asked me Dan'.

Dan sat up, 'is that right woman? Well okay will you marry me, Mary?'

'I don't know much but I think I recall something about kneeling and having something in a a box.'

Dan chuckled and lay down, 'well okay woman, soon as I can manage it, I will do it right.'

'Yes Dan.'

'Yes what?"

Yes, Dan, I will marry you, you know it.' She elbowed him softly.

Dan laughed softly and Mary felt a shiver go right through her. She loved his laugh.

'Dan, you have nothing to be sorry for. I felt beastly for letting you think Jack was .... You know.'

'Mary....'

'Dan' Mary cut him off 'don't ever ask me. Don't ask me who Dan. I won't marry you if you can't promise me that. Promise me that Dan. It is over and done with. I dealt with the bastard Dan.'

'Alright Mary if that's what its gunna take. Mary, I came here last....'

'I know Dan, I know. But I knew I was in...... knew I was going to '

'I could have helped you Mary you don't need to go through these things on your own. Remember darling, never be afraid and never be embarrassed.' Dan kissed her, 'It's over Mary, we'll go on and have other girls. I love you with all my heart Mary. I need you darlin, need you to be alright. I need you.'

'Oh Dan' Mary's arms went round him, and he kissed her long and tenderly. All he ever wanted was her arms around him. He'd put his back to the plough, by God he would.

Outside Noreen heard a faint laugh and she smiled. Her heart felt better.

Inside Dan pulled Mary to him and held her tight. 'Mary, I brought the baby home, and I thought if it's alright with you I would like to bury her down beside your parents. I loved her Mary you know.'

Mary held his face in her hands and said softly, 'I know love I know. I did to. Oh Dan, that's a lovely idea to put her to rest with Mum and Dad. I would have been about four and a half months Dan. I wish I'd told you before but....'

'It's alright Mary. Do you want to be there Mary?'

'Yes, I do Dan.'

'What about Ben and Noreen Mary? And any others who want to come? Everyone is sad Mary and very worried about you. You know they all love you don't you. Can they come Mary? It's entirely up to you.'

'That'll be okay Dan just as long as they don't come because they feel they have to.'

'I'll make sure they understand that and thank you. I sort of need them there, we need to acknowledge our little girl, Mary.' Dan sniffed and getting up on one elbow he kissed Mary long and lovingly.

'God, I love you Dan. I will get up a bit later on and we could bury her tomorrow.'

'Should we give her a name Mary?'

'I suppose so Dan. Do you have a name in mind?'

'Yes, I do. We will bury her as Grace. Grace Mary Smith Roberts. What do you say Mary?'

'Oh Dan, it's perfect.'

The following day they buried their little girl beside Mary's mother and father. There wasn't a dry eye there. Dan had dug the grave and had put together a small box as best he could. Mary hardly spoke.

Noreen was worried about Mary fearing this was too soon. But as proceedings went on, they could see that Mary was doing what she needed to do. A priest came from in town and blessed the small girl and later spent some time talking to Mary.

Dan could see it was what she needed. The priest had assured the young woman that God was watching and that her baby was with God now.

After a while the priest took Dan aside and told him that he thought they had done just the right thing. That Mary had absolution and so did the baby. 'Do we know who did this Dan' he asked?

'No, we don't Father.'

Chapter 9

There were many potatoes to harvest. Summer was just round the corner, and they would plant vegetables that would grow in the hot conditions and keep well in the cellar. They had also planted by the river in case they had to water the gardens. Onions were almost ready and carrots, turnips, and broad beans.

The men had returned from the river with fish they were getting ready to smoke and the boys had brought home two rabbits. Wally and Dan had gone out to see if they could get a pig.

Dan had money put by for a rainy day now and he loved it. Whenever the people who worked gave him money, he hung on to what he could which was most of it. They were making a little money selling their surplus vegetables to and they had taken to planting enough to be sure they had plenty to sell. Dan worked tirelessly at the gardening and sometimes they sold fish and rabbits. People were hungry and food was scarce everywhere. Mary and Dan would go to the market every month and sell everything they had. Dan found that he loved it. Loved the excitement he felt in his belly.

The older men had made plates and dishes and forks and spoons from wood, even stools and small tables and they sold these to. They were very popular. They also smoked fish and rabbits for the market. The townspeople found that the community added a zest, an energy to the markets and almost the whole town turned up now. They knew they'd get food they could afford and some utensils to. They were mighty glad to be able to get them and they had begun to see the community people in a new light. Knew they needed them.

Some to the young men had gathered building materials from the dump and had started adding a lean to onto the house for families to sleep in. It would free up more space for the families and for tables and stools. The space they would vacate would probably sleep two or three families.

The people of the community had not forgotten the starvation they had experienced and were glad they had Dan. He managed the money and had never been selfish or greedy. They knew he was honest, and kind and they loved him.

Dan brought the people together at the dinner table almost every week to talk about things they needed, and money would be handed out for these things.

Some of the women were trying to get decent clothes ready for the children to start school. They also knew that Dan was saving the fees to send the kids to school and that made them feel almost normal. They loved their long house and took good care of it.

Out of the money that Dan handed them back they bought curtains and bedding for the long hut. 'It's starting to look absolutely lovely' Noreen said one night. 'We have bright colours now Dan. And the kids love it, and they have friends come over sometimes. Kids from town Dan, who would have thought?' They also bought clothes, Dan himself had two new shirts.

Mary had told Dan that the lambs would not be ready for a couple of months.

'When they are we should kill only one at a time.'

Dan studied her face; she still had a haunted look on it and he supposed she would for some time. 'How do you feel about it all Mary?' He'd asked her gently.

'I don't know Dan, I just don't. On the one hand I am broken on the other she was not conceived in love. What am I supposed to feel?'

Dan kissed her and held her as she cried. It was one hell of a situation; he didn't even know. But that he had loved that little girl was true. He knew they would have both loved her regardless. They had only just buried her a couple of weeks ago so he supposed it would take time.

And here he was today stalking a pig with a gun. Young Wally wasn't a bad shot he'd leave the killing to him. Dan had lost his heart for it since he'd looked upon a half formed little girl. He'd get Mary to see Noreen when he got back.

She needed the extra support.

Wally pulled him to a stop, and he was brought up out of his musings. There in front of them was a pig munching on roots. They desecrated so much ground the bloody things. He handed the gun to Wally and shook his head. Wally understood but he was alarmed. He knew he wasn't the best shot, but the pig was close.

The younger man lifted the rifle to his shoulder and took aim and held his finger on the trigger. He held his breath and his finger on the trigger. He lowered the rifle from his shoulder and looked at Dan. He couldn't do it to the big fellow, he'd seen him brace himself. Wally shook his head slowly and returned the safety. 'I'm sorry Dan, I just can't mate.'

Dan smiled at him, 'well we're a great pair. What are we gunna take home lad?

To eat?'

Wally studied his feet for a while and looked up with a smile. 'I guess we'll have to eat the same as we did when we first got here. Do you remember that first night Dan when Mary brought us all those vegies? The women cooked us a bloody stew and we had damper to eat with it, how bloody good was that?

Well, we are lucky to have a cellar full of fish and rabbits, and vegies, aren't we?'

'Yes, we are son, and we did think those vegies were pretty damn good, didn't we? I will never forget it, Wally. What it felt like to be starving and to watch those you love starving to. Especially the little ones, mate that was just bloody heart breaking. There were times I thought it would surely kill me.'

'We owe Mary so much Dan, I wish there was something we could do. I have never been sadder than these past couple of weeks Dan, never. And the funeral was...... Sorry Dan.' Wally sniffed, 'and what she must have gone through alone Dan '

'Me neither Wally. I was looking forward to having a baby girl to cuddle and play with as if she were mine. Mine and Marys. It would have been the communities and we all could have shared her and the joy of her. I will marry Mary someday Wally.'

'You gave her a beautiful name Dan and you gave her your name. That's huge man.'

The two men trudged towards home. Dan sniffed the air, there was rain coming. He loved the rain now though in Melbourne he had done nothing but complain about it. He said this to young Wally now and they both laughed.

'Yeah, you see things differently in the country don't you Dan? You learn about nature and food and animals and stuff. And now you are going to be a proper farmer Dan. Are you looking forward to that?'

Dan laughed, for the first time in weeks he laughed heartily. Clapping Wally on the shoulder he said 'yes, I am Wally. I love this life, this place. You know I think I'll stay here forever. You know Mary has made it clear that whoever wants to stay is welcome to. That three acres we are on shall not be taken away from us.'

'What? Forever Dan?"

'Yes, Wally forever. If you want.'

'Yeah well, I'm staying, I never wanna see that damn city again or smell it or hear it. I saw the ganger yesterday and he said there will be an opening in the railway gang soon, in a week or two. Says he'll put in a good word for me.'

'Good on you son' Dan looked up towards home 'maybe the boys got a duck or some such Wally.'

———————

Dan climbed up on the cart beside Mary, it was a cool morning and Dan was excited, he took the reins from Mary. Today he would climb back into a truck all be it a small one. Mary chatted away beside him and as he looked at her, he smiled. 'Mary let's never get rid of this cart. Promise me Mary. I fell in love with you in this bloody seat sneaking peaks at you from the corner of me eye.'

'Oh Dan' she snuggled up to him and he almost dropped the

reins. 'I could never get rid of it or Lilly. We'll go on picnics in this and take the kids. All of them. You know I have fallen in love with all those kids Dan. I can't wait to see them all off to school.'

Dan put an arm around her and kissed the top of her head. 'I know woman. They all love you to. Damn it Mary, everybody loves you' Dan gave a chuckle, 'well maybe not everyone.' Dan tightened his arm around her, the grin slipping from his face. 'One day Mary I'll find out who that bastard is, and I will kill him. I'm not asking you to tell me I know you won't, and I know why you won't. But I will find out.'

Mary slid out from under his arm and sat quietly for a way. Dan cursed himself for the fool he was. 'Sorry Mary' he said at last, 'you know I am sorry don't you Mary.'

'Shut up Dan.'

'Okay Mary.' Dan took her hand in his and when he saw the tear slide down her cheek, he had to swallow hard. He squeezed her hand gently and pulled the cart up under a tree.

'Oh, come on Dan, let's just get on with it.'

'No honey, I have made you cry now what can I do to get back in your good books woman.' He turned now pulling her into his arms, wiped her tear with his hanky. 'Talk to me please.'

'You know what is wrong with me Dan. If you kill someone, they will hang you and then where will I be and the boys? Well Dan? Where?'

Dan sat for a moment unable to speak. At length he said 'you want me to forget it, Mary? Forget what that mongrel did to you?'

'Yes Dan, that's exactly what I want. Promise me Dan.'

Dan swallowed hard several times, he just couldn't take it in. Just forget it. But he wasn't willing to make her a promise he wouldn't keep. He sat back and looked at her. He looked around at the countryside and wondered why nothing came to him. No words came to him, he felt like he'd been winded.

Slowly he took his arms from around Mary and got down off the cart. Walking to the head of the horse he took the rein and walked the horse for about five minutes. Stopping he turned and looked up at Mary. 'You expect me to do nothing Mary? Just let it go. Let the bastard get away with it?' His voice though loud held a quiver.

'That's about it Dan. I want to be married to you, get old with you. Not watch you hang or rot in prison. I'm not interested in any of that. I understand how you feel, and I must say to you now, I will not marry you. I will never sleep with you or love you and that way you don't have to feel as if you have to kill someone. Get in the cart Dan and let's get the bloody truck. We can still be friends and business partners. Dan! Get in!'

Dan stared at her open mouthed and gulped. 'Mary, you don't mean it. For Christ's sake woman tell me you didn't mean any of that.'

'I mean it Dan. You don't have to go throw your bloody life away doing something you feel honour bound to do. Either get in or get out of the bloody way and I'll get the damn truck by myself. I'm not going to discuss this shit anymore.'

'Jesus, you curse like a navvy, woman. You will marry me, and I will not kill anyone. Now Mary that's the bloody end of it.' Dan turned around and walked that horse and cart almost all the way to town. Dan was sulking and he knew it but to say such things. The outskirts of town came into view.

Dan was feeling confused and sorry for himself and when he felt the riding crop across his backside, he sucked in a good deal of air. He felt hot tears spring to his eyes, and he grabbed his backside and turned and looked up at Mary. Searching her face for pity he gave it up soon after, she stared coldly back at him. 'Stop the damn horse Dan.'

Dan stopped the horse and going around the side of the cart he dragged Mary down off it. He was breathing heavy, his bum hurt like hell. He looked into Mary's face, and she started laughing. 'That's what you'll bloody get if I find out you've been asking questions in town. I want all this to go away for good do you understand?'

A chuckle started deep in Dans' throat and erupted into a belly laugh. They clung to each other for a time and laughed heartily. Dan turned serious now, 'why didn't you do that back there woman.'

'I thought I might just let you walk for a while. I like watching you walk.' Mary turned serious now, 'I mean it Dan, you promise me, or I will never marry you. This is all I ask Dan.'

He kissed her and lifted his head to look into her eyes. 'Yes, woman you have asked me for damn all and given me so much. So, I give you my solemn promise I will not go looking for your attacker. And, in the event that I accidently learn his name I will not kill him. This I promise you dear, on the lives of my children I promise you this. Now Mary, are we to get married?'

'Yes Dan.'

'And are we to go and get the bloody truck Mary?'

'Yes, we are my darling. I'm sorry I hurt you.'

Dan pulled her close and kissed her tenderly. 'Do you still have that blanket up in the back there Mary?'

'No, I don't. Let's get...'

'The bloody truck, I know.'

Dan helped Mary up into the cart then climbed up himself. He sat very gingerly on the seat and took up the reins.

———

As the harvesting of the vegetables went on the women got to work and dried and pickled using wine vinegar. They smoked fish and rabbits, though the fish and rabbits weren't likely to run out, they did sell a lot of this pickled dried and smoked produce at the market. Mary had donated one of her goats to be killed, she couldn't keep it, it was a male and she couldn't kill it either. Mary didn't know if she'd ever kill anything again.

The older men got to work and cut it up and their half they dried and smoked some of it and the women made a lovely roast out of the leg. The rest of it was cooked in a stew. It was almost November and Mary, and Dan were getting ready to harvest the wheat.

'We'll get some practice Dan' Mary smiled over coffee as they sat in the kitchen at the long hut.

Dan sat staring at the woman who had stollen his heart as he was wont to do. He smiled and said softly, 'We probably should Mary, December is going to be wet. I know this because I heard it on my radio. The one my girlfriend bought for me.'

'Should a girl be jealous of this girlfriend Dan?'

'A girl should be very jealous and never think to see old Dan around the traps again. He is taken Mary.' Dan lowered his head for a moment and stood up indicating she come with him. Outside he walked away holding her hand.

'What is it, Dan?'

When they had got away out of sight in the trees, he turned to her 'Mary I cannot stand this.'

'What Dan?"

'This Mary. You come over and we have to sit in front of everyone across the table from each other. I want to marry you Mary and be with you night and day. Do you hear me, Mary?'

'Oh Dan, I want that to darling. But we must wait an appropriate time… '

'What is an appropriate time Mary' he stared at her, and she dropped her gaze? 'Come on Mary tell me. Then I'll know…. Mary.' He walked away from her a bit and with his back to her he said. 'This is not an excuse is it, Mary? You do love me, don't you?'

Mary stepped close to him and taking his hand she turned him to face her. 'Please Dan, be sure you never ask me that again. We just need to give it a little more time. What do you want to do Dan?"

'For Christs sake Mary, I want to sleep with you.' He took her in his arms and kissed her lips and then her cheek and her neck. 'I need it, Mary. I need you.'

'Dan let's get the harvesting done.' Mary tried to push him away, but it was half hearted at best, 'please Dan. Not here. Help me Dan, let me go. You know I find it almost impossible to refuse you.'

Dan lifted his head to look at her and smiled 'do you Mary? I love you woman. Tell me when Mary. A month? Two?'

Dan looked at her and noted the distress and the need in her and let her go. He bent forward and kissed her lips. 'Alright Mary, I shall go on waiting for you. What about tomorrow night Mary, can I come over and see you?'

'Of course, Dan, you know you can.' Mary put her arms out to him, and he came to her. He had a great need for this woman. He lay his head on her shoulder and smiled, one day he mused. And he'd wait by Christ he would. He wanted only this woman, no one else would do. No more of that running around looking for something in other women that wasn't there. He had it all right here.

Mary was talking again, 'come for dinner Dan. I'll make you some dinner and you can ...... you know...... You can start courting me if you like.'

'Well alright Mary. Let the courting begin be God.' He smiled, 'now you are my girlfriend, Mary. Officially.'

———〜〜∘◦❀◦❀◦❀∘◦〜〜———

A week later, Dan got up onto the tractor and started it up. This was it, make or break time. He looked across at Mary sitting on the fence and waved. She waved back and clapped her hands. Everyone was there watching, and Dan's heart pounded, God he hoped everything worked. He cast a quick look at Ben who nodded his head and smiled. Dan slipped the tractor into gear and pushed the throttle. He let the clutch up and drove slowly out into the crop.

Samuel, an old farmer, and Mary had decided on the height and so after a few yards he stopped while they checked it. They nodded their approval to Dan.

Mary jumped up and down and squealed. 'Everything works Dan, even the catcher. It all works!'

Samuel and Dan laughed; it was good to see her this way again. Dan patted the wheel arch and Mary climbed up and sat, still laughing, beside him. When she leaned on his shoulder and put her arm about him, he felt a joy in his heart.

This was in front of everyone. This was progress. And they were driving a tractor! They were harvesting their crop, the one they had sewn with Lilly. Dan felt a tug at his heart. There was Lilly standing by the fence with all the kids, watching. He realised with a jolt that he loved that bloody horse.

Samuel walked along beside them keeping a watch that the catcher was working, the whole thing fascinated him. They'd need every grain to have a proper Christmas and send the kids to school. Some of the mums had gone into town and finished getting them clothed and shoed and started getting them pencils and such. They had to have a set of pencils each and a lunch box and a bag for the pencils, Dan had said. There were eleven of them starting school, six boys and five girls and in Dans eyes they were all capable of being prime minister someday. They had to be well set to go to school.

Dan also wanted them to have a small school bag each. He didn't know why but it was important to him. It was about status and standing and all that. He worried about these kids under his protection being below the others, being below anyone. Being teased and ridiculed. Nope, they had to have a school bag to put their lunch and their books and pencils in.

After the harvest, Dan and the men got busy bagging the wheat. The bags were heavy so only Wally, Dan, and Mathew lifted them onto the truck. The older men got busy sewing the bags, as always it was a joint effort. Dan knew how important it was to these older members of their community to be still useful. Contributing to a project like this would give them a much needed lift.

Dan and Mary took the wheat to the silos in the truck, Dan liked driving the truck but he was glad to the heart of him he didn't do it for a living now. He loved this farming life that he shared with Mary. He could never imagine himself doing anything else now and found the thought of living life with out the woman beside him to be simply unbearable.

———◦◦◦◦◦◦◦———

It was Christmas eve and Dan had made sure all the children had a toy wrapped up and under the tree, a toy of pretty near equal value. He and Wally had gone out and cut a limb from a conifer tree down near the town dump and carted it all the way home on their backs. Dan said that blue gum just wouldn't do for this occasion. Some of the older girls had decorated it with pretty crepe paper while some cut out paper shapes to be hung. Things were working out nicely and they were almost ready for the kids to go to school in just weeks.

Mary and Dan had cut hay and thrown a lot of it up on the cart, tonight they would harness Lilly up to it and go into town. The children, up on the cart, would sing carols as Mary drove around the streets. Ben drove the truck along behind the cart with all the men on board.

Dan looked at Mary now as she drove the cart along to town. 'How do you think they will go Mary? No one has taught them Christmas carols and such.'

He'd never seen the kids so excited, so he kept his voice down. Mary did the same as she smiled at him. 'Noreen and some of the other mums and I have been teaching them Dan, they sing beautifully. Just wait and see.'

And Dan did see, they sang so beautifully that it brought tears to his eyes. They were all dressed up in their Sunday best, all wearing their school shoes and new socks. 'It'll help to wear them in a bit before school,' said Dan. Some of the kids had gone barefoot for so long that Dan planned to get them to wear the shoes every day for ten minutes. He knew what a mess new leather shoes could make of tender heals.

The kids had one of Mary's lambs up on the cart with them. Some of the boys wore towels and held sticks to act as shepherds. Only the best towels were brought out and used for this occasion. Dan and Mary were proud of them, even the little two who were three sang heartily. Mary sang with them. All the people from the commune were there and wore huge grins. There was a humble pride about these people now.

Towns people turned out to listen and fell in behind the cart with Noreen and the other people from the community. They were all there, and they all joined in the singing after a while. Mary pulled the cart to a stop in the town square where the monthly markets were held. A crowd was gathering.

An old man brought out his accordion and began to play silent night and the children sang along with him. They sang some more carols along with the beautiful music. It was beautiful and towns people shook hands and introduced themselves to these, once homeless people whom they had at first shunned.

The children began to jump down from the cart to play with the children from the town. Dan was flabbergasted, Mary had done it again. He'd been dubious they all had but Mary had ploughed on, and there were not many who would say no to the little she asked. The kids had enjoyed themselves immensely and now the adults on both sides were.

It seemed that everyone forgot their troubles and enjoyed themselves for a while. Dan stood next to Mary and soaked up the music and the laughter. The magic that only Christmas could make.

Josh the schoolteacher was there, and he approached Dan and Mary where they stood talking excitedly their faces aglow. 'Hello Dan, hello Mary' he said as he walked up to them. 'I must congratulate you both on your splendid show and a thoroughly enjoyable evening. Next year we could maybe include some of the school children, they would have loved this. I must say how much I admire the fact that you go all out to bring joy to your youngsters.' He put his hand out and Dan shook it.

'We haven't always been able to and it's only thanks to Mary here that they weren't singing on foot.' He laughed nervously; Dan was basically a shy individual.

Mary shook hands with the young schoolteacher also and said, 'I would have had nothing at all if it weren't for these wonderful people. All I brought to the table was the horse and cart and yet I had a wonderous evening. Yes, next year we may be able to make it a joint effort. The kids are having so much fun, all of them. I saw some of the town kids singing along to.'

'Well, they all sang beautifully, and they are all so polite and bright. I cannot wait for next year. I have been watching them and I notice that most of them are in the higher grades....'

'We lost a few.' Dan said simply and left it at that.

'I'm so sorry Dan' Josh murmured, and Dan smiled softly at him.

Noreen walked up at this moment and the teacher smiled at her, 'have you any children coming to our school next year?' He wished he could keep his mouth shut as he saw her face fall.

Noreen smiled and said, 'yes we have two who will be attending.'

Josh took a deep breath, 'aren't you a nurse.... er.... Noreen, isn't it?'

'Yes, it is and yes I am Josh' she smiled.

'Well, we are always short of nurses at the hospital Noreen. If you have some hours, you could contribute we would be grateful, I'm sure. And may I say the pay is good Noreen.'

'Thankyou Josh I would certainly like to earn.'

'Well see the matron as soon as possible.' He turned to include them all and said goodbye to them. Noreen got a silly grin on her face.

'Oh yeah,' said Dan, 'we will miss you around the house Noreen.' Noreen and Dan smiled at each other. Dan could see the excitement building in her and he was pleased for her. He looked serious now, 'we'll need a horse or some such Noreen. I don't want you walking to and from that hospital at all hours, it's over a mile, it's too much after a shift.'

—⁓⁓⁓⁓⁓⁓⁓⁓⁓—

Dan woke up on Christmas morning to someone shaking him. He looked up, it was Mary. He looked around him and noticed that those he could see were asleep. He reached out and pulled Mary down on the bed beside him. She went to speak but he kissed her, 'hush woman' he whispered pulling the blanket up.

'Dan please' she started. He slipped his arms around her and held her for the briefest moment. His heart nearly stopped. He had the love of his life in his bed with his arms around her. His heart got going and soared.

'Alright, alright darling I just wanted to see what it will be like.' He was breathless.

He let her up and when she stood beside his bed gazing down on him, she said 'well?'

'That was the most beautiful moment of my life so far. Now get me a coffee woman, before I forget I'm a gentleman.'

Dan sat quietly with Mary at the table savouring the coffee she made him and just being alone for a bit. Ben came over and pretty soon everyone was up. It was bedlam. Once all the kids had their present, they raced outside to play with it.

Most of these kids could never remember receiving a present and unwrapping it, couldn't remember ever having a toy. In fact, that bat and ball they made was the only one Dan could remember since they'd hit the road. Dan could feel their excitement. They all got what they'd asked for, Dan had gone by train to Mildura to get the presents with a list and a bag.

Most of the adults had tears in their eyes as they watched the kids squeal with delight at their toy. Some of the older girls had got a purse and the boys got a pocketknife. They were happy. They had bought presents for everyone up to the age of eighteen. One of the girls was nineteen so they had got her a present.

The women then turned their attention to preparing the food. They had a turkey a goose and two chickens. These would all be roasted and served with stuffing, vegetables and gravy.

A week before Christmas one of the boys, Mathew, had asked to bring his girlfriend to the dinner. Dan had put it to the dinner table one night, and it had been decided the girl would be welcome. She was introduced to everyone as Sarah.

Dan was once again impressed by the dinner table. There had been a second table made and placed alongside the other one. Now almost everyone could sit down. A smaller fold up table had been introduced and was brought out for meals. It was a low table and the children sat on a mat on the floor. A stool along the wall was used by anyone who missed out on a place at the tables.

The larger table was laden with the meat and vegies and fruit. There were two puddings and two cakes. A lot of food didn't get eaten but it would be packed away for later. When they had finished eating the adults sat around talking quietly and Mathew asked if he could speak. Dan nodded to the young man.

Mathew got to his feet and cleared his throat a few times. 'Thanks Dan. All I want to say… well to ask really is Well, your blessing Dan. Me and Sarah want to get married. Now the thing is…... that er…… we would want to live here. See Dan, Sarah's parents don't approve of me, and they have made it clear that she will no longer be welcome at their home if we marry.'

Dan turned to look at Mary who got up to get a cup of tea then turned back to the couple. 'Well congratulations Mathew and you to Sarah. It is sad that your parents feel that way lass.' Dan smiled softly at the young couple; Sarah had got up to stand beside Mathew. Dan waved his hand and said, 'sit down the two of you.' Dan realised in that moment that he knew very little about Mathew. The boy was so quiet and withdrawn.

Dan got to his feet and found he didn't have to call for silence. Most people were smiling kindly at the two, Mathew and Sarah. He glanced at Mary who stood off to the side away from the table. He couldn't read her face, so he began, 'I think young Mathew that we all are the extent of your family. So, I don't know where else you would go. Even so I must be sure that everyone agrees so I 'll put it to the vote. All those in favour of Sarah and Mathew living here?'

The 'yes' was unanimous around the table and there was much congratulating went on. Dan glanced at Mary and raised his hand for silence. 'Before we get carried away folks, one of us has not yet voted.' He was looking directly at Mary now and all eyes turned to Mary.

She looked at Dan, 'me Dan? What has it to do with me?'

He never took his eyes from her face and couldn't believe it as he watched her squirm. 'It has to be unanimous Mary. We cannot bring another into the community if you don't vote for it.'

There followed a most awkward silence and then Dan said softly to the young couple 'I'm sorry but I think we need more time. We may address this again farther down the track.' He all but collapsed back in his chair.

Mary came and stood at the table, 'I'm sorry I just wasn't expecting this. May I vote yes Dan?'

Dan looked up at the woman he adored, the woman who had been so good to them, had saved them all from starvation had saved lives here and given them a comfortable home. He smiled faintly at her, how he loved her. But this was a shock. He spoke kindly to her. 'No Mary you may not. We will however, if you like, redo the vote in a week. Is that alright Mathew?'

Mathew didn't answer straight away he was trying to conceal something. Dan knew it, Ben had seen it and so had Noreen. Noreen felt sick in the pit of her stomach she wasn't sure why. She looked at Ben and knew she didn't worry for nought.

'Well, that concludes this business for now' Dan sat in his chair still staring at Mary.

But Mathew wasn't finished and now in a defiant tone he spoke straight to Mary. 'Why can't she come here to live?' He shouted now 'Why?'

Dan got to his feet and so did Ben and Noreen. Ben got out from his stool and edged towards Dan.

Mary stared at Mathew and, like someone in a trance, said quietly 'why didn't you help me?'

Dans eyes narrowed as he switched his gaze to Mathew. Mathew was squirming now his face red. 'I don't know what you are talking about' he retorted.

Mary leaned on the table towards the young man and spoke in a harsh voice. 'You were there Matt. I saw you, you watched, and you didn't lift a finger to help me.'

'What the hell' Dan stepped back and nearly fell over Ben. Ben put his arms around the big man prepared to hold on for dear life. Dan made to move towards Mathew but couldn't. 'Ben, get out of my way man'. He looked at Mary desperation all over his face, 'Mary, tell me what goes on here.' He had the presence of mind now to say 'someone get the kids outside.'

Maynard and Samuel did the honours. Noreen came round the table to Dan now and spoke beseechingly to him. 'Dan please don't spoil the day for the kids, you'll hate yourself for it.'

Mary spoke as if just coming out of a trance, 'Noreen's right Dan, you have my vote now I had best leave.'

'Mary no…. wait. Jesus Christ Ben, get out of my way. Just stay calm I'm not going to spoil anyone's day but his' he pointed his thumb at Mathew. His temper was rising as the situation began to dawn on him.

Mary was at the door now and Dan said 'Ben if you don't shift, I'll bloody hurt you man. I need to talk to Mary.'

Ben nodded and stepped aside but he shepherded the big man to the door. Dan ran out as Mary dashed past on her horse. He grabbed the reins and pulled the horse to a stop some yards away. When he got Lilly calm, he pulled Mary from the horse.

'Please Dan, I'm sorry. I'm sorry Dan.'

Dan put his arms around her and held her, 'hush now woman you have nothing to be sorry for'. She was shaking from head to foot. He stood and rocked her gently in his arms until she calmed. He lifted her face to look at him and said softly, 'what are the two things I told you to never feel with me woman. One was fear the other embarrassment. Now you have my word Mary that I will not go off half-cocked no matter what you tell me. But if it's what I think then that kid has to go. Hay? Come on my love, tell old Dan what goes on. What did he watch Mary?'

As far as Dan had tried to brace himself, he sobbed when she told him that on the night, she had been brutally raped, Mathew had watched on through a window and then had turned his back and walked away. And Dan had given his word. He said quietly now 'you want me to go and throw him out Mary?'

Mary looked at the ground and then up at Dan, how she loved this man. Dan saw it in her eyes and smiled down at her. 'Could you take me home Dan? Please baby.'

'I must show this man off the property Mary and see that the girl gets home safely. You must see that sweetheart. Come, you can watch that I don't do anything stupid. And I really don't want to spoil this day anymore now.' He took her hand and led her inside calling to Lilly as he did.

Back in the kitchen he led Mary to Noreen who held her. Dan turned to Mathew and tried his best to keep his voice even. 'Mathew, I think it is obvious that you need to get your things right now and go.' Dan saw Mathews eyes slant to Sarah. Dan said calmly, 'Sarah, I will take you home to you parents.

What you do from there is your business, but I must see you safely home from here, what are you seventeen? Go on Mathew go. There is no place for such a callous coward here.'

Dan took a five pound note from his pocket and handed it to Mathew and handing him another two shillings he said 'this'll get you on the train to Mildura, they are hiring men on the highways there. Get out of town Mathew.'

Mathew got his things and spat at Mary as he was leaving. Dan went to step forward, but Mary stopped him. He said quietly, 'alright, Mathew if I see you again after this, I will put you in hospital.'

'Yeah, well that's because you're gunna take her word as usual.'

Mathew left the house and walked off down the road to town. Dan walked outside to watch him go and the men gathered around him. Dan looked at them, 'I hate letting him go, he's trouble.' Dan rubbed his chin, 'we must stand guard on Mary from now on. Keep an eye out in town and if you see him let me know. I'll go along there to Marys and sleep at nights from six until six.

Wally you and Ben take turns to do the days. And I say you Ben because now I know if you get him in a bear hug, he is fucked.' The men all laughed, and the tension was eased.

Mary heard Dan laughing with the men and she breathed easy again. Noreen had her arm around Mary, she was thinking the same as Dan that she didn't know much about Mathew. She had noticed that when there was work to be done, he'd sort of melted away with the kids, made himself busy minding the kids. Noreen wasn't sure if Mathew was capable of living by himself, but they could no longer let him stay here. Still, it was upsetting to throw one of their members out like that.

Noreen looked at Mary, how much had this young woman to go through?

Dan came back in the door and went to Mary, 'come on love, it's all over. We'll talk about this soon for now I'll take Sarah home. I'll be back soon to take you home and I won't leave you alone this night.'

All eyes turned to Sarah, she just looked bewildered. 'Are you alright' Dan asked? She nodded.

Dan went on, 'look Sarah if your parents don't want you back, I shall bring you home with me. One of our number has brought you to this so you have a home here if you need it.'

Sarah smiled, 'thank you Dan' she said quietly.

Chapter 10

*D*an had taken the girl Sarah home and dropped her at the door. He noticed that her parents were curious and so he told them that they had asked Mathew to leave and thus had brought their daughter home.

'Well thank you very much young man, Dan, isn't it? We do hope he stays gone, we never wanted our daughter to marry him.' Her father shook hands with Dan and smiled at Sarah.

'No dad I'm no longer interested in marrying him. And thank you for bringing me home Mister Roberts.'

'You are very welcome. I am sorry for what has happened to you and by one of our members. I hope you will forgive us, we brought him among you' Sarah and her parents assured Dan there was nothing to forgive and thanked him again for seeing their daughter home.

'You can't always know' the old man said sincerely. He liked the young man who stood in front of him. He'd heard a lot about this man Dan, and none of it had been anywhere near bad.

Dan had hurried off home to take Mary home. He spotted Mathew sitting at the railway station and decided to sit and watch. Dan didn't think there were any trains today but maybe he was waiting for one the next day. He hoped so. Mathew put his bag on the seat and lay down on it, yes maybe he was waiting for a train thought Dan. And maybe not he sighed.

Dan turned the key and hit the starter button and started the truck up. He shoved it in gear and left, he'd promised Mary. He needed to get home to Mary, he was suddenly tired, it had been a huge day. He drove all the way home fighting the urge to go back and give that mongrel a good hiding. But his Mary was worried about him. He smiled softly at the thought.

Back at the compound he bundled Mary into the truck and kissed his boy's good night. The kids were all still having fun. 'You get into bed when Noreen tells you.' He looked around and smiled, it did his heart good to see the kids all playing with toys. He would do his best to see to it that they all got a toy for their birthdays as well. There were fourteen kids eleven school age and three under five. There were also three kids who were not yet eighteen.

On the way home he told Mary someone would be with her all the time until he was sure Mathew was gone. Mary looked across at him and then slid across the seat to sit right next to him. He took his hand off the wheel to hold her to him. 'Do you wanna park up Mary? Wanna fool around a little?'

He felt her arms go round him and he was pleasantly surprised. 'Maybe just a little Dan. Are you doing the night shift honey?' She hugged him tight.

Dan hit the brakes and stalled the truck. 'Gunna let me under that blanket woman?' Mary giggled and held the rug up.

'Hang on, you haven't got that riding crop under there Mary, has ya?'

'Oh yes Dan, I has. You got work to do you has.' He put his arms around her and pulled her to him. He was laughing, Mary was laughing and Dans world was right again as he lay her down on the seat.

———— ⦁⦁⦁⦁⦁⦁ ————

In mid-January Mary received a cheque for almost two hundred pounds for the wheat she and Dan had taken to the silos. She went to the bank and withdrew one hundred pounds and went to see Dan. She'd got the one hundred in twenty, ten, and five-pound notes.

Mary walked into the kitchen and found no one about except

Dan who was asleep at the table. She shook him awake. 'Mary, what a lovely surprise woman. I'll get you a coffee.'

'Just a minute Dan I have news. The other day I got a cheque for the wheat.' Dan looked surprised and smiled. 'Good Mary.'

She smiled at him and pulled the wad of notes from her bag. 'Your share Dan just like we discussed.' She watched the look on his face as she counted out the money. He was amazed, Dan had never seen so much money. Not for him.

Mary went on now, 'I know you will put it with the money for the community Dan, but the others all keep some for themselves. Keep twenty for yourself Dan. You are going to need some new dungarees anyway.'

He sat staring at the money. Nodding his head, he said 'you know Mary I believe I will. I'll keep two twenties and I will begin a savings account at the bank.' He grinned at her. 'I will put some money each week in it and out of the rest of this Mary I will get new work clobber and some new boots. We will get those bags for the kids to.' Dan looked thoughtful 'can I borrow the truck this afternoon Mary?'

'Of course, you can Dan. You have no need to ask.'

'Imagine Mary, next year when we have planted eighty acres.'

'Yes, Dan imagine, I'm so looking forward to ploughing this year. With you Dan and the new tractor, I can't wait darling. But I think we have to visit the market this week, don't we?' Mary got up and fished five pounds out of her pocket and placed it in front of Dan. 'For the bags Dan, for the kids. Let me Dan, if you want to argue about it, I'm quite capable of doing that for the rest of the day and most of the night. You know it's useless Dan. I love those kids and I always intended to get their damn bags.'

Dan picked up the five-pound note and sighed, 'thanks Mary. I love you woman. This will get their damn bags Mary.' Mary watched with a smile as he picked up his cash and put if carefully into his wallet.

———∿∿∿◦◦◦◦∿∿∿———

The next day Dan pulled up out the front of Marys. She was sitting at the table doing some sewing. Dan sat down and watched her for a while then, 'what you going to do with your share Mary?'

'I'll put it all back in the kitty love, all except for five pounds, I'm gunna spend five pounds on myself. We are making around ten pound a month each at the market to Dan.' Mary watched him fidget, he had a funny look on his face.

Suddenly he got up and came round the table and pulled her chair about to face him. He knelt down in front of her and produced a little box. 'Will you do me the honour Mary? Of becoming my wife?'

Mary had to laugh but she slid off the chair, kneeling in front of him she threw her arms around his neck. 'Oh Dan.'

'Is that a yes' he grinned as he took the small ring from the box and put it on her finger.

'It's the most beautiful thing I have ever had Dan and it's a yes.'

He hugged her to him. 'Mary, I love you so much. I have waited for this day since the first day I saw you. I knew Mary. I knew I would move heaven and earth to get you. Knew I had to have you. That first day you waved and rode off I knew I needed you. Needed to learn what you could teach me. And I dared to hope Mary, hope that I wouldn't be too dumb to learn.'

He stopped talking, Mary was staring at her ring, 'don't you like it' he asked gently?

'Oh yes, I love it baby. It is beautiful and I have never had anything like it. I will treasure it all my life. But how did you know what size Dan?'

'I tied a string around you finger while you were asleep.' Mary laughed and he laughed with her. He was happy but his gut was in a knot, he'd just seen Mathew, large as life in the street.

'So can we tell people about this, or should I wear it round my neck under my clothes?'

'Whatever you feel comfortable with my love. Where's Ben?'

'He went fishing Dan, he's just down at the river there.' Mary put her sewing away and stood up. 'Are you here now Dan or do you have to go back to the compound first.'

'No, I'm here now woman.'

'Have you eaten baby?'

Dan walked up to her and took her in his arms, he held her close. 'Nay woman, I love your cooking. Will you feed me Mary? Please?'

He turned back and sat at the table, 'I'll just wait here. So, Mary, are you gunna make me wait and see what you decide concerning wearing your ring?'

Mary smiled and came to him slipping her arms around him she sat on his knee. 'Think I will wear it Dan. But maybe not in front of the boys huh?'

'Well Mary, Kane demanded to know what the hell I was doing about making you mine, asked me what the heck was I waiting for. I said Well you can't rush these things.'

Mary was laughing and she said, 'well I guess I'll wear it. What about Bryce?'

'Well Bryce told me I was too old for you and that I should leave you for a much younger man. I said "what, one of about six years of age Bryce?" He went red so he wants you for himself Mary. The little blighter wants to cut me out.'

Mary and Dan were laughing when Ben came in the door with three fish. 'For your dinner Mary. So, I can get off home now Dan? I'll walk if you don't mind thanks. It's a lovely walk and it clears my head some. I go down along the riverbank, it's lovely and cool.' He walked to the door and turned, 'that river has come to mean a lot to me. Can't imagine life anywhere else now. I have come to love fishing to. Well I'll get going you two.' He smiled at them and turned to go.

'Okay' said Dan and followed him out. Out of earshot he told Ben about seeing Mathew in town.

Ben lowered his head and shaking it now he said, 'I never knew what to make of him Dan, he always seemed sort of guarded. I believe he was capable of doing what Mary says and even though he's not much more than a kid he could have done something. Even if it was just to run home and get us. But he did nothing Dan. And he stood watching the fuckin little creep. No, you did the right thing Dan. Do you think we should take a few of the lads and go find him and drive him to Mildura in the truck give him a good hiding and drop him there. We shouldn't have to live in fear because of him. That woman shouldn't have to live in fear Dan. Not Mary, not any woman.'

Dan smiled at Ben, 'yeah that is exactly what we should do. But we won't tell Mary about the hiding part, okay?'

It was three days later before Dan and his band caught up with Mathew. There were Ben, Wally, Samuel, and Maynard with him. They spotted Mathew walking along Main Street and they followed him until he turned down a quiet street. Dan drove up a little ahead of him and came to a sudden stop. Before Mathew knew it the five men were out of the truck and had him surrounded.

'What do you lot want? Come to tell me to get out of town I suppose. Well, you can't tell me what to do so you can all get stuffed. It's a free c....'

Dan picked him up and threw him in the back of the truck where he started yelling blue murder. Wally was up in the back and delivered a solid kick to his ribs and Mathew stopped yelling.

'You just shut your mouth' hissed Wally. 'You are gunna see what happens to people who don't get out when they are told to get out.'

Maynard and Ben jumped up in the back and sat on Mathew while Wally sat near his head. 'Just make another sound and see what happens' he said.

Dan jumped in the front and Samuel got in the other side. They sped off and took the highway out towards Mildura. After they'd gone about halfway Dan pulled the truck up off the road a bit. They all got out and Wally dragged Mathew out. When he was standing looking at the five men around, he asked 'what are we doing here? You all gunna leave me out here in the middle of nowhere.'

Wally held Mathew's arm on one side Ben on the other. Dan stood in front of him and delivered a blow to his midriff. Shaking his head Dan asked the two men holding him to let go of him and when Mathew got his breath he said, 'you may defend yourself Mathew' then he went about giving the young man a hiding he'd never forget. When he was finished, he was breathing heavily. He hated doing this, hated it with a passion. It left him feeling sick. There was a time he would have enjoyed it but a lot had happened since.

Then the other four got him and hoisted him up in the back of the truck. Wally sat him up and held his head up as Dan spoke to him. 'Now Mathew, we are going to drop you off in Mildura. If we see you back in Baltana or anywhere near it, I will take you out in the scrub and kick you to death. You vile mongrel, you walked away from a woman who was being brutally raped, a woman who handed us back our lives. You are nigh on twenty Mathew you know what's what. Then you thought to ignore us when we gave you the chance to run. Did you think you'd just walk away from it you arrogant little bastard? Thought you'd just keep strolling around town wiping our fuckin noses in it?'

Dan pulled his fist back, but Wally stopped him. 'You think he's had enough' asked Dan?

'No mate I would like a shot.'

'Of course, Wally go for your life.'

Wally punched him and so did Ben. Wally turned to Dan 'now he's had enough.'

Dan got back in the truck and started it up. They drove Mathew to within two miles of Mildura and dropped him in the dirt by the side of the road and Dan repeated his threat. 'You can walk from here, Mary had to get herself up, get to our place and then she did a full day's work. Don't ever come back Mathew'

Dan told him as they drove off and left him.

In the front of the truck Dan knew they'd done the right thing. They'd shown that little mongrel and any other of his type that there were consequences, dire consequences. To anyone who thought to come into his camp and treat his large family like they were not important. And to think that this was one of their own!

Well, now Mathew knew better and if Jack ever came back, he would need to toe the line. Dan always got a pain in his heart when he thought about Jack. He wondered where he was. Dan was certain that war was coming, from out of Germany most likely he thought.

———— ᘓᘖᓂᕬᘓᕬᓂᕬᘖᘓ ————

Back on the highway wally let out a hoot and the others did to. They looked back and saw Mathew had made it to his feet. They all doubted that he would come back for more of what he'd just had. Dan had even produced the riding crop and lay it across his bare backside.

Mathew had screamed and Dan gave him a second lash. That's when Mathew had begun to sing.

It was nearly dark when they got back, and Dan dropped the men off spent some time with the boys and said good night to them. He spoke briefly to Noreen and went straight to Marys.

She was waiting nervously and went straight into Dans arms and held him. 'Tell me he is still alive Dan.'

'He is Mary, we slapped him about a bit and left him at Mildura. Of course, I told him if he ever returns Mary, I will kick him to death.'

'Would you do that Dan?'

'Well, he believes I will Mary, he believes it.'

Mary sighed; she hoped Mathew believed it. Dan knew Mathew would never want to cross swords with him again he was basically a coward with no gumption as well as no guts. He told Mary this now 'we will still watch over you at night Mary, for a while' he grinned at her. Looking a bit sheepish he said, 'well I've got used to the good tucker you dish up.'

Laughing now, Dan picked up this woman that he loved and headed for the bedroom, glad the day was over.

Dan also knew how much that riding crop hurt, and he'd used it with a bit more force than Mary had. Mathew had screamed alright.

He'd smuggled the thing back into the veranda he thought he probably wouldn't mention that to Mary. 'So how many times Dan?"

'What darling? How many times what?' Dan stopped what he was doing.

'You know Dan, how many times did he get the crop around his backside?'

'Jesus' woman, you swear like a.......'

'Navvy, I know. Wanna go and get it and I'll liven things up a bit.'

'No, I don't Mary and we'll have no more of that sort of talk.' Dan kissed her then lifting his head, 'unless I get to use it. I know what you're like.'

They both laughed, Dan lay beside her and held her gently in his arms. 'I love you woman. I see you are wearing your ring.'

'I am Dan.'

'Why didn't you tell me Mary?"

'Dan I just wanted it all to go away.'

'You should have told me Mary. You....'

'I had no one Dan. You were still married and you had enough on your plate, I couldn't Dan.'

'Oh Mary, there I was crying on your shoulder.'

'It was different Dan. You were losing someone you loved.'

Dan sat up and looked at this woman he'd lost his heart to. 'Mary you mean the world to me, you have done from the first. The day I met you and you handed me so much. But you took so much to. When you rode away you had my heart with you. And you know something Mary, I never want it back. I fell for you that first day. And every day since its gotten stronger and deeper.'

Dan made love to Mary and he felt an ecstasy he wouldn't even have dreamed of. He held her to him all night and thanked God there in the darkness for her.

Chapter 11

At last, the big day had arrived, the children were off to school. Everyone piled into the truck and the cart to deliver these most precious of their number to school. The children were dressed up in their new clothes and their nice shiny shoes. They wore their school bags on their backs with their lunch and their pencils in there. Their hair shone and so did their eyes. The adults were wearing their Sunday best as well.

Dan had smartened himself up, he had on his new shirt and his new boots. But he was nervous. He didn't want to be late and was relieved when he heard Mary arrive in the cart. The kids piled into the back of the truck the smallest sat in the front with Dan. He was so proud he could hardly breath. He had meticulously cleaned the back of the truck so the kids up there wouldn't get dirty.

The people of the compound found somewhere to sit in the truck or in the cart. Of course, there was Bryce sitting right next to Mary, Dan smiled. Then the whole troop set off for town. Joshua waited at the gate and could hardly believe his eyes as the procession rounded the corner and pulled up at the front gate. No one got out until Dan had shaken hands with Josh and he turned and nodded.

Josh suggested he take the children to sort out which classes they would be in. Because of the fact that they had been away from school for a time they would need to do some testing. 'To be absolutely fair' he smiled at Dan. He was impressed by the easy manner of the man and the way that children and adults alike seemed to love him. He'd be an amazing teacher thought Josh, he had an air of authority about him that was so natural you overlooked it.

Dan was talking to the kids now, 'you go with Mister Vance here and do as he tells you. And mind your manners all of you. Now go ahead and say your goodbyes.'

Each of the kids hugged each of the adults even the old fellows. Most of the adults looked teary eyed while the old fellows openly wept. After he softly told the old men to pull themselves together, Dan spoke to Josh, 'Where might a man pay their school fees' he asked?

Josh was a little taken aback, he hadn't expected it. 'There's no hurry Mister Roberts.'

'The front office?'

'Yes, yes of course. Those buildings over there.' Josh always felt like one of the kids around the big man. 'You can get them enrolled while you're there. Just tell the ladies in the office we'll get back to them with the grades. And then they'll be given their books accordingly.'

Dan thanked the man and kissed the children telling them he'd be there when they got out. Looking at the small children he told them gently not to forget to eat their lunch. 'You are young men and women now and you shouldn't need to be told' he smiled down at them. Then he and his entourage strode off to the office to pay the fees. Josh shook his head and smiled as he ushered the children towards a building, if all the parents were like him.

He'd heard a rumour of one of the men at the compound falling foul of this man. If the story was correct the man was a very unsavoury character, one they wouldn't want hanging around the town. But Josh had also heard that the last time this man had been seen was when Dan and some of the others had thrown him in the back of the truck and carted him off. He hadn't been seen again.

Dan's justice was swift thought the young schoolteacher. And what fate, thought Josh would befall the man who did this horrendous thing when that quietly spoken man got hold of him? And who among them could blame him and more to the point who among them could stand the mongrel who in all probability, was the one who did it?

The talk around the town was that Dan would be perfectly within his rights and the perpetrator himself had heard this talk. And the two who assisted put as much distance as they could between him and them. When the police sergeant heard the talk, he sank into his chair and put his hand to his face.

Dan and the mums got the children enrolled and paid the fees. As they walked back to the truck and the cart, Dan felt a contentment settle on him. The fees were half what he had reckoned so they had money left over. The kids were in school at last.

Times were only getting tougher out there and Dan wondered where they'd be if it hadn't been for Mary. He had come to love their long hut and wondered how he would leave it when he and Mary married. He pushed it from his mind and took Mary's hand as they walked along. How he loved her. He had to find a compromise where there could be one. Other things that twisted his gut during the night, there could be no compromise for. Promise or no.

———✦✦✦———

A few weeks later Wally started on the railways and found himself working with Ron. Dennis had got the job of paymaster and worked in an office at the station. He had enjoyed walking to work with them that morning. Dennis got off work about three thirty and he scooted round to the school to walk home with the kids.

Wally and Ron walked home together later at four fifteen. They were walking along the road when Dan came upon them and picked them up. Wally got in the front.

He looked at Dan and said 'some of the blokes were talking today mate. Something came up about councilman James being carted off to hospital. I'm not saying it was you, and if it was, you should've come and got me. All I'm saying is that it's out mate. That's all Dan.' Wally went quiet for a moment and then 'don't think the police will come though, apparently he's not talking.'

'Thanks Wally' Dan said quietly.

'I don't blame you Dan. Is that it now mate, or are there others we need to deal with?'

'It was him Wally' Dan said. His tone brooked no argument.

Wally sighed and sat back in the seat.

———⟋⟍⟋⟍⟋⟍⟋⟍———

Dan arrived at Mary's place to find her in the yard, she watched him get out of the truck her face a thunder cloud. 'Hello, my love' he said and held his arms out to her.

She ignored them. 'You know I went into town yesterday, Dan?'

'Yes, baby I know that. Did you get everything done?' Dan walked past her into the house, he thought he knew what was coming and decided to take it in the back.

Mary followed him inside, 'One of my friends told me she'd seen council man James the day before being carted off to the hospital. Said he looked like a horse stomped on him.'

'I didn't hear that Mary, is he alright?' Dan sat in a chair and pulled a reluctant Mary into his lap. 'Come on woman, what has this to do with us?'

'No Dan he isn't alright. Did you have anything to do with it?'

'What, you mean the beating Mary?'

'Yes, Dan the beating that put him in hospital. I know it was you.'

Dan pushed her off his knee and stomped towards the door. He was brought about when she yelled his name.

'What' he yelled back.

'You lied Dan. You made certain....'

'Promises Mary? That is correct and I broke none of them. My promise to you was that I would not look for him and I didn't, I didn't have to look for him Mary. I also promised that I would not kill him, and I didn't.' He took a step back towards Mary his eyes narrowed 'Blind fuckin Freddy would know it was him and your face the other day proved it.'

'He's in hospital from the beating you gave him. Where are you going?'

'What about the beating he gave you and the.... the other. I never gave him a beating Mary it was aversion therapy. Now I'm going, I'm not Gunna stay here and be treated like a bloody kid. Don't you treat me like a kid Mary.' Dan wiped spittle from his chin and took a deep breath and walked to the door. He turned in the doorway and yelled, 'what did you think Mary? What did you think I was gunna do? What just let the mongrel come in here and brutalise my girl and just let him get away with it? No Mary, no. He came and took my woman the mongrel. And what of the others Mary? Am I to stand by like a bloody kid and watch as those bastards come and pluck one of the girls from right under my fuckin nose and do the same to her? Which one Mary? Which of our beautiful, young girls is next? Would you like to choose? And then they'll come for another and another.... Well not if I can help it. Fuck em, they can't do whatever the hell they like in my camp to my people, my family, and they cannot do what they like to you. I'll see you later Mary.'

Dan didn't sleep that night; he'd sat all evening hoping she would come and speak with him. Forgive him, tell him she understood. Maybe even put her arms around him and hold him. He was hurting. Yes, he'd given the mongrel a fair going over but he hadn't killed him, and God knows he'd wanted to. It's not like the mongrel hadn't deserved it.

Dan got into bed at midnight and tossed and turned. At four o'clock he gave it up and got out of bed. He got a cup of coffee and went outside to sit on the log and drink it.

Someone sat on the log beside him and he knew it was Ben. 'How much damage you reckon you done young un?'

'I dunno Ben, I dunno. She expected me to do nothing and let those bastards think they can come in here and help themselves to our womenfolk on a whim. Well, now they can think again. The other two will be shitting themselves.'

'You going after them to Dan?'

'Well, I didn't do what I did to Mathew to let these bastards off Scott free. They did worse than he did. One of these two is going to finish telling me exactly what went on.'

'Well then don't go on your own Dan. Take one of us with you at least.'

Dan looked at Ben, studied his face and realised with a start what a comfort the man had always been. And Dan realised that he was usually if not always, right. He put his hand on Ben's shoulder now and smiled, 'I won't go too far Ben. I have no desire to do life.'

'Well just remember the people here are counting on you son. Are you gunna go and see Mary, I'll wager she is doing just this Dan except that she has no one to talk to.'

'Maybe Ben, but she wants me to say I'm sorry and I am not. I haven't finished with them Ben. Who will those bastards come for next if I sit and do nought?'

Ben couldn't answer, the possibility had occurred to him to. He drew a deep breath; the situation was terrible. He rose to his feet, 'see Mary son.'

Mary had not slept, she had waited for Dan to come back to her, to take her in his arms and tell her everything would be alright. Well, he hadn't, and the sun was coming up.

Mary got dressed and put her boots on, she had to remain productive so she got her fishing gear, some traps and some lunch and left the hut. At the doorway she reached into a pile of blankets and grabbed her handgun and a box of shells. Mary was halfway to the river when she realised that Dan was right. He was absolutely right but she was terrified she would lose him. She'd been carting her gun around ever since, but she told herself it was because she might get a pig or a turkey.

She had her handgun with her because she was afraid, they'd come back again.

It hadn't occurred to her that they might be after one of the others. And this with Noreen starting work in a weeks' time. She had been selfish. And what if it was one of the young girls they snatched. She realised that instead of opposing Dan she should be helping him.

But Dan had yelled at her and walked out and for him to do that she knew he must be really angry. She bowed her head and trudged on downstream. She heard a footfall behind her and swung around, it wasn't Jim he was up ahead. She pulled her gun from her pocket and cocked it as she turned. It was Lilly, she flung her arms around the big horse's neck and cried. Lilly dropped her head and held the woman's back until she stopped, 'Oh Lilly what have I done? Oh, never mind my beautiful friend I am probably just tired.'

Mary walked on to her favourite fishing spot; she had set three traps along the way. Setting herself up on an old deck chair she left here she baited her hook and threw it in the water. Almost instantly she got a bite and threw the line back in. When she'd caught three fish she cleaned them and put them in some water.

Mary didn't know how long she'd been asleep, but Jim was growling. She jumped to her feet and looked in the direction he was. Suddenly the big dog gave a yelp and fell to the ground and Mary heard a shot. She yelled 'Jim, Jim Oh God Jim.' Mary forgot all the training from her dad and ran to the dog. He was breathing and trying to sit up. She had to quiet him and get him to stay down, he was bleeding.

Mary suddenly wondered who would do this? Jim looked up at her and snarled and she knew she had been too careless. 'Drop the gun bitch' a man snarled.

Mary did as she was told she knew he had a gun to her head. Another man stepped out of the trees in front of her his gun over his shoulder. These were the two men Dan was looking for.

The man in front of her spoke, 'we just want to have a talk Mary' he sneered.

'You didn't have to shoot my dog you mongrel.'

The man whose name was Rodney laughed. 'No? Anyway, it's about that boyfriend of yours. Did you hear what he did to James?'

'Yeah, and he'll do the same to you as soon as he....'

Rodney had delivered a stunning blow to the side of her head. 'You think so? Well see you are going to stop him. You tell him if he tries the same with me, he'll bloody regret it. I'll go to the police. I'll go to the bloody mayor.'

'That's a good idea Rodney that'll stop his gallop. Just as soon as you tell these people why he's after you. Tell the mayor how you violated Mary Smith.'

A viscous look crossed Rodney's face and he took a step closer to her, when he spoke his voice was a low growl. 'I'll shoot your fuckin dog. Call the bastard off Mary, this is your final warning. I'll start with your fuckin dog and then your fuckin horse and then we'll shoot your man. Then we'll start picking off the folks in the camp, they're bloody scum anyway. We didn't fuck you, James did and who's gunna believe that he did? You and your scumbag friends are gunna be in a lot of trouble.'

'Well first of all if you believed that you wouldn't be here, and you and your buddy did help him. And secondly, everyone in town believes you all did it. Didn't know that did you, that everyone knows?' Mary smiled at him now and said 'anyway you can talk to him yourself. He'll come running when he heard that shot.'

Now Rodney smiled, 'no he won't we just watched him go into town.'

Mary felt her hopes plummet, what if they decided to shoot Jim? She changed tack, 'you seem to hold all the aces Rodney, now what is it you want?' Dan wasn't coming. Maybe he never would again, Mary felt sick.

'Well, I dunno Mary, you're just a bit lucky I wouldn't touch you after them fuckin inbreeds have been taking turns with you.' Rodney lifted his gun and pointed it at the dog's head.

'Please' Mary screamed. Her mouth fell open as Wally dashed out from behind a tree and in a few seconds, before Rodney could turn, had reached him, and belted him so hard in the side of his head with his fist that Rodney was dazed. Wally took the gun and removed the bolt and put it in his pocket. The man who was holding Mary let her go and started backing away. Wally advanced on him and the man started stammering, 'it wasn't my idea, I didn't want to come. I'm sorry.'

Wally took his gun and kicked Rodney in the midriff, 'and yet here you are. You move and I will shoot you.'

Rodney glared at Dean, his accomplice and sneered, 'why didn't you shoot the bastard. You got no balls.'

'No Rodney we can't just shoot people because it suits us. No, fuck you I'm out.' He looked at Wally 'you won't get any trouble from me mate.' He sat down under the tree.

Wally looked at Mary and handed her, her gun, 'you, okay?' Mary nodded and went to the dog. Wally looked at it and said 'Mary I think it's just a flesh wound. He's lost a bit of blood though Mary we need to get this bound up.' He turned to Rodney, 'Give me your bloody shirt.'

Rodney stared belligerently at him and just as Dan drove up he smacked Rodney and took his shirt. He ripped the shirt and bound the dog's shoulder.

Dan looked hard at Mary and spoke not a word; he had things to do. Hunkering down he tied Rodney's hands behind him. Not bothering to keep his voice down he hissed 'you are fucked now Rodney.' Looking up at Wally he smiled, 'I probably heard the same gunshot that you heard.' He stood and walked towards Dean, 'I've been looking for you blokes, nice of you to come and save me the trouble.' He tied Dean up to and then lifted them with Wally's help and threw them into the back of the truck. 'Thanks Wally, I hate to think what this mongrel would have done if you hadn't got here….'

'I want a word Dan' he took the big man by the shoulder and walked away a bit Leaving Mary nursing Jim. 'Listen, I got here and hid behind that tree over there, Dean there could have given me up any time, but he didn't, I think he's frightened of the other one. Rodney here had a gun to Mary's head. I heard the mongrel threatening Mary that if she didn't stop you from coming after him, he'd shoot her dog her horse you and then he'd start picking us off at the camp. Just so you know Dan and also, when you cart these two off to deal with them, I'm coming with you.'

Dan looked aghast at the young man before him, 'a gun to her head Wally? You think they've been threatening her all along Wally? Jesus! I'd like you to stay here with Mary.'

'No Dan, here's what we'll do. We'll take Mary and Jim back to the camp and to Noreen. We'll pick up Ben and Maynard and head off up the creek and give these blokes a little of what you gave James. Bring the riding crop.' Dan nodded and went to turn about. Wally grabbed his arm, 'And we'll do all this directly after you've had a word of two or three with Mary. They shot her dog Dan. I'll put the dog in the back with me, you and Mary get in the front. Come on Dan.'

At Mary's instruction she got dropped at her hut, 'Better if I look after Jim here.'

Dan stopped the truck and came round the back and said to Wally, 'it's what she wants. Hand Jim down to me' he glanced at Rodney. 'You are going to regret this; you can't just do whatever you like. I'm gunna teach you some manners.'

Dan carted the dog in the back door and Mary asked him to put him on the blanket she'd put on the floor. 'Mary….' He started softly.

She broke in harshly, 'yesterday I would never have dreamed that anything would make me regret knowing you. Loving you as I did. Today I don't bloody care Dan, you go do what you want.' She sidestepped his hands 'just go please.'

Dan stood in the doorway. 'Are you sure Mary?'

'Yes Dan, I'm sure. It's too hard to love you, it's too hard.'

'I'll come back after... '

'Don't bloody bother Dan. I blame myself; I should have gone to the police, but they seldom actually do anything.'

'What do you want me to do Mary? Please Mary, what?'

'See this, Dan? This is the reason I didn't want you involved. I hope you are happy. It's over Dan, it's just over. I told you I would never marry you if you did this.' With that Mary stood up and took her ring from her finger. She gazed at it and let the tears fall. Handing it back to him she saw his tears. 'I'm sorry.'

'I have things to do Mary. These bastards took what was mine and thought they'd come back and just do whatever the fuck they want. They held a gun to my woman's head and threatened her. I have to make a stand Mary, else they'll keep coming, I know these bastards. I'll be back Mary, I'll be back for you. I have children in that camp, I have to try and protect everyone.'

'I know, I know that now. Well go on Dan. We will still go to the market this week and then we will not see each other socially. I will stick close to home and that way I won't get hurt. So, I will see you bright and early on Wednesday.'

Dan stood in the doorway looking down at the ring which Mary had just put in his hand. Hot tears ran down his cheeks and he wiped them away roughly. He looked beseechingly at her and turned and left.

Dan went back out to the truck, he felt sick. He'd grabbed the riding crop from the veranda and got in. He drove slowly back to camp and sat in the truck while Wally went to get Ben and Maynard.

When they dropped the two men back on the outskirts of town their backs were bloody. Dan had taken hide off with the riding crop. Rodney had begged the loudest, his back was far worse than Deans, Dean had been let off lightly compared to Rodney.

Before he left them Dan said to Rodney, 'we have a witness to the whole rape. If I see you anywhere, I will take Mary to the police. How long have you been threatening her?'

Rodney was sobbing so Dean answered, 'he's been standing over Mary since the beginning. Since he suspected you might know. James doesn't know he's been going out there.'

'Right' said Dan turning back to Rodney, 'listen up. Wally heard all the threats you made to Mary. You blokes are just bloody stupid. If you know what's good for you you'll get out of town. Come near my home or my people again and I will kill you.'

Dan went back to the camp and told the others to get out of the truck, he had to go see Mary. At Mary's place he didn't look to talk to her but took the riding crop down to the river and washed the blood off it. He took it back and hung it in the veranda.

He knocked on the kitchen door and Mary appeared. Dan strode past her and went to Jim, 'how is he' he asked? Turning to look at Mary he said 'he gunna be alright?'

Mary nodded. 'What about you Mary are you alright? I'm just asking.' She nodded 'yes I'm okay.'

'I put your riding crop back where I got it.' He turned and left. Just outside the door he said , 'I have killed no one Mary. I still haven't broken any of my promises, but you have Mary. I will not break any of my promises to you.'

Dan got back in the truck and went into town. He parked the truck in the hospital car park and entered the building. He had to be careful, he didn't want to spoil things here for Noreen. He very politely asked a nurse at the desk where he could find James and she told him.

James was surprised to see him and started yelling at him to get out. Dan sat beside his bed. 'Now see James, there are a couple of matters I would like to speak to you about. Now, did you know James that Rodney and Dean have been visiting Mary for some time now?' James shook his head, alarm registering on his face. 'Well James they have been coming out there to threaten her and stand over her to get her to make me back off. Did you know that, James?'

James looked down and shook his head, so Dan went on. 'Well, here it is James, they came out there today and shot her dog. We have witnesses to what you have done James and to what they have done.

A young man in our camp watched you all that night, through a window. These witnesses are going to write out an affidavit. I am not going to put up with anymore of this. I'm off to see the mayor. You have committed crimes that will put you away for twenty or so years.'

'What about what you have done?'

'Now see this is what I mean. Do you think that brutalising a young girl is okay? You show no remorse James. I got hold of your friends and let them know how disappointed I am in them. I will take these affidavits to the prosecutor's office and see what he suggests hay? Your main whistle blower is one of your own.'

James shook his head 'I'll see to it that this all stops Dan.'

'Alright James that is a good decision because if you don't I will.' Dan made to rise and sat back down. 'I almost forgot James, you and you buddies will do one of two things. You will resign from council and anything else you're in and leave town. Or you will all transfer out to the city. A copy of these affidavits will be lodged with my solicitor in case you think you can get rid of this. Now do I have your word?'

James nodded and started to cry, 'I promise…. I promise….'

Dan walked away. James sat in semidarkness and watched as his friends were wheeled down the ward. If the mayor got wind of this.

As Dan walked through the hospital doors to the outside world he took a deep breath, his jaw was set, and a tear slid down his face. He never knew the tall heavily built man on his way in who said hello to him was the mayor of Baltana.

———⁓ɷɷɷ⁓———

Dan got back to Mary's place about an hour before dark. He knocked on the door and waited until she came to the door. He handed her the keys and said quietly, 'do you need anything Mary?'

Mary shook her head 'no thanks Dan. You wanna cuppa Dan?'

He smiled sadly and stepped inside and went to Jim 'no thanks Mary. How is he?'

Mary stood beside him, she was close, so close. 'There are no broken bones, and he is eating and drinking. Dan, I can't find Lilly' her voice broke.

Dan's blood ran cold, 'where did you see her last Mary' he said softly?

'At the river today. I caught a couple of fish and went to sleep. When I woke up, she was gone, and those men came and shot Jim.'

'Alright Mary, give me the keys and I'll go and look. Where have you looked for her?'

She told him and ended 'I didn't really worry until about an hour ago. But she's always home before this.'

Dan went the opposite way to where Mary had looked and hugged the riverbank, stopping now and then to call her and listen for her. He was getting a panic feeling in his gut. He stopped about half a mile down river and turned off the motor. 'Lilly... Lilly' he called and listened. Then he heard it, a soft whimper from the big horse.

Dan ran to it and stopped dead. There was Lilly tied to a tree branch overhanging the river, in the water. Her head was almost submerged, and she had to hold her head back to breath. Dan grabbed the knife from his belt and with fading light dived into the water. He cut the rope and helped the horse as best he could to dry land. He threw his arms around Lilly's neck.

Leaving the truck where it was, he walked home with her, and she stayed close to him. It was dark now and just a few yards from home, Lilly put her head back and whinnied. Mary ran to them and hugged her horse.

'Why is she all wet Dan?'

'The bastards tied her in the river. A rise of one foot and she would've drowned.' Dan gave a great sob and sat on the ground, he looked dazed, defeated. He sat getting his breath and Mary held him. She could feel him shaking.

Then Dan got slowly to his feet and walked off into the dark. 'Where are you going' she called to him? 'You are all wet to Dan.'

'To get the truck Mary. To get the goddamn truck.' He took a couple of steps and turned 'see to your animals Mary and I will bring the truck back in the morning. Two shots Mary, two shots.' He melted into the darkness and Mary had to stop herself from calling him to come back. Begging him to come back.

Dan found it hard to walk away from Mary in the state she was in but he needed to be by himself for a while. Despite what anybody might think he despised himself for the things he'd done lately. He hated violence but these bastards had struck at the very heart of him. They had hurt Mary so they had to pay.

When Dan got home, he told Ben and Wally briefly what he had done finishing with rescuing Mary's horse.

'That bloody Rodney is a sick bastard' blurted Wally.

Ben gave the big man a cup of hot coffee and said softly 'How do these people dare. They think they are above the law?'

'We'll still have to be careful. What do we do if the law comes looking, should we get an alibi ready. Like each other?'

Ben nodded and said 'it might be best Dan.'

Wally sat up, 'We should work on it Dan. Me and Ben will start writing down the times we were out doing this stuff.'

Dan nodded and smiled at Wally, 'yeah, we'd best start working on our story mate.' Though Dan was more than sure they wouldn't need to.

Ben looked hard at Dan noting the hangdog expression and red eyes and said softly, 'and you and Mary Dan?'

Dan shrugged and Ben felt his misery. Dan swallowed his coffee and went to his bed. He passed out as soon as his head hit the pillow. He dreamed of holding Mary's hand down by the river while the boys played with the dog downstream and his heart beat nice and steady.

Chapter 12

*D*an knocked on Mary's door the next morning at sunup. 'I brought your keys back Mary.'

'Come in Dan' Mary got them a cup of coffee and put them on the table. When they were both sat down, she sipped her coffee.

'You make the best coffee Mary. Now what's on your mind?'

'Is everything alright Dan…. With you?' Her voice was small, and she looked tired.

'Yes Mary.' He took a gulp at his coffee. 'Alright Mary, I guess you are just worried.' Dan told her briefly of his trip to the hospital now. 'Mary you are not to blame yourself. And you should trust me a little more. But anyway, what's done is done.'

'Dan I can't drive the bloody truck so…… Well take it and come pick me up on Wednesday.'

'Alright Mary. Would you like me to teach you how to drive it?'

'I guess we'll have to work out what we are now and what is left of our life. I can only say I am sorry Dan. Anyway, we can leave that for another day.'

'Alright Mary.' Dan got up and thanked her for the cuppa. 'I'll see you Wednesday then. Remember Mary, three shots.'

Three shots Mary thought sadly as she listened to him go.

———◦◦◦◦◦◦———

Dan waited every night for Mary to come but she did not. He sat at night and listened to the radio and tried to feel the love that had been. On Monday night he threw his hat at it and went to bed, and he didn't turn it on again. Ben sat and worried, mostly with Wally. They all missed Mary.

Wednesday morning Dan loaded the truck and headed off to get Mary. He told himself along the way that he'd have to be content with this now.

Unbeknownst to him, Mary was telling herself the same thing.

She waited outside and fussed about what she had to go on the truck. Satisfied with it Mary sat on a box and picked up a stick and began to scribble in the sand. He'd offered to teach her to drive the Goddamn truck. She smiled and then frowned, could she? Then what?

She was deep in thought when he arrived, and she swung around and once again the sight of him seemed to catch in her throat. She got up and started throwing bags and boxes up on the back and Dan helped her.

As they drove down the road in silence Mary decided to take the plunge, 'yes Dan. Thankyou.'

'For what Mary?'

'Well, you offered to teach me to drive.'

There was a long silence and he said somewhat flatly 'good for you Mary. No really, good for you. I'll be glad to teach you. You can get your licence Mary.'

Mary looked at him and he looked at her. She wanted him with every fibre of her being. She dropped her head 'I shouldn't have treated you like a kid.' The tears rained down her face. Dan stopped the truck and stalled it.

He reached across and pulled her to him. 'Does this mean I am forgiven Mary?'

He held her to him.

She nodded her head, 'pretty sure you are supposed to put your foot on the clutch when you want to stop Dan.' He laughed softly. 'Can you forgive me Dan, that is the question?'

'Oh, woman please don't. I love you, Mary.' His lips came down on hers. They both sat up, 'we need to get to the market,' said Dan. 'Righto' said Mary.

Dan's head swam all morning at the market as they kept sneaking smiles at each other. And that day Dan made eight pounds ten and six. Mary made six pounds one and threepence.

During the course of the morning, people he didn't know hailed him and some introduced themselves and shook his hand. A couple of them mentioned how good it was that somebody had finally stood up to the bastards. 'Your produce is second to none to young man' they'd say. Dan learned that they called James the sheriff of Nothingham.

Dan and Mary picked up the things they had bought for home and got in the truck. They both knew what was going to happen on the way home.

Dan pulled the truck up at the ice cream shop. 'Come on Mary I want to buy you an ice cream.'

They were on the way to Mary's house after dropping off the things for the long hut there. Halfway Mary slid across in the seat and slipped her arms around him and kissed his neck. Dan stalled the truck.

———❦———

Mary was digging in her vegetable garden, she had planted more tomatoes, she had some seeds for fast-growing bushes. They were getting a very good price for tomatoes and Dan was doing the same. It was almost halfway through February and the tomatoes would be ripe for next market. She couldn't admit that most of her motivation was to keep her mind from all things painful.

Things had gotten back to normal, and she and Dan were taking it slowly. Dan had made no move to give her back her ring and came to see her only a few times a week. So, Mary had decided she'd best start getting over things as best she could. She did this by keeping largely to herself and working hard. She knew there were things she had to get over now that the worms had risen from the can. Mary didn't know she was suffering from depression.

She was deep in these thoughts and the big black car was almost upon her before she noticed it. Mary felt her gut knot up as she waited to see who it was. The car stopped and a tall man got out, it was the mayor. Oh no, thought Mary, what now? She dropped the shovel and walked towards him removing her gloves. She tried to keep her composure, but the worry lines were deep in her face.

Phil the mayor was saddened by the sight of her. He put his arms out to her and she hesitated before she stepped into them, he had always hugged her when she was little and he came to see her father. He held her for some moments then stepped back to look at her.

'What is it' she asked? 'Why have you come?' Her voice sounded resigned, she looked resigned. Phil felt tears in his own eyes at the question. He was taken aback at the change in the once happy go lucky girl he'd known for years. He told himself after what he'd heard he shouldn't be all that surprised.

'I should have come way before this Mary, but I lacked the guts. I have the story, mostly from Dean, and I am mortified Mary. Can we sit down for a while my dear, you know chew the fat.' He raised is hands now, 'I am here only to apologise Mary, nothing more.' He saw her relax.

When they were seated with a cup of coffee Phil began. 'I heard the story going around about James and I found it hard to believe, even for him. I questioned him and he told me that this was the community putting it around because he told them they had to leave the commons, which I would never have done Mary. I dug a bit farther and found that by this time they were all living on your land.' Phil stopped and sipped at his coffee, 'you always did make good coffee Mary even when you used to make it for me and your dad. Last time I saw you was his funeral; how do I apologise to him?' He sniffed, 'for not looking after his daughter.'

Phil lowered his head and Mary couldn't see him properly. He sniffed and raising his head, he went on. 'I felt that James wouldn't have had the guts to go out there on his own, and he wouldn't have. Then I hear that he had help out there and I knew then that it could be so. Oh, Mary I am sorry, so very, very sorry. The next thing I heard was that you had a miscarriage, and I questioned the priest. He looked me straight in the eye and said he could not tell me anything and that he was duty bound to keep anything, no matter how terrible, confidential. He went away wiping his eyes and that was when I knew.'

He sat still, looking at Mary. He had loved this girl since she was tiny, yet he had failed her so badly. Couldn't have failed her worse. He said helplessly, 'Why didn't you come to me Mary?'

Mary sat still, she just wished he'd go. 'I am getting on with my life. I don't want anything to happen to those people because of me. That's all.'

'And nothing will Mary. I'd like to think that I would have the guts to do what Dan did, but I doubt it. He had a perfect right to look out for his loved ones else who knows what those bloody clowns would have done. No Mary I have no beef with him or any of the others. I saw him walk out of the hospital that day Mary and he looked haunted.' Phil swallowed hard, 'if you need anything Mary, come and see me. The three of them have left town, I believe Dan threw them out and I knew he acted in your best interest. I told them the day I saw Dan at the hospital, that if they came back, I'd have them locked up.'

Phil finished his coffee and asked Mary to see the graves of her parents. 'I see another little one Mary. He is quite a man, Dan Roberts, quite a man.'

He hugged Mary before he left and went on his way. Mary had promised to come and see him if she needed anything.

———·····———

The next day Mary went into town to pick up her mail and some wheat for the chooks. She stopped in at the general store to get some coffee. She got some lollies to and turned to walk out. At the door she said hello to Kathy one of the girls from the community. Kathy worked at the school two days a week; she was about the same age as Mary.

Kathy smiled sweetly at Mary and said 'have you heard the news, Mary? Dan and I are engaged to be married. Look, isn't it lovely?'

Mary looked and her heart split in two. There on Kathy's finger was her ring, the one she'd given back to Dan. No wonder she thought bitterly, no wonder he hadn't given it back to her. No wonder he only came round now and then. Mary knew then she'd need to learn to drive that truck pretty damn quick for when he married her, he'd have to leave. She knew she couldn't stand that. Couldn't see those two about all the time.

She got on Lilly and set off at a gallop, Lilly knew the way home. Mary cried for days. Dan came round on Monday for her lesson in the truck, but she refused to answer the door.

Then one day Mary caught Dan getting in the window and grabbed her riding crop. She brought it across his chest, and he jumped back out. 'Mary, Mary what is going on here? Have you heard Mary? Mary.'

'Oh yes Dan I've bloody heard alright. How could you Dan? How could you? Go on Dan get going.' And with this Mary brandished her gun.

Dan started walking backwards. 'Please Mary, it's not that bad. I'm sorry l....'

Mary let off a shot. 'Leave the truck Dan, I'll teach myself the rest. I never want to see you again and, if you come here again, I will shoot you on sight. How about that you low down rotten sod. Clear off or I'll shoot you.' Mary let off another shot this one took out the lantern just above his head. He turned and walked away and cried all the way home.

Almost a week after and still not seeing Mary, Wally walked across there. He had to try and see her and find out what was wrong, Dan was a mess. The man had cried for days he never slept and ate very little. Wally suspected he'd been drinking at one stage.

Wally hid behind some trees and waited. Eventually Mary came out to feed the animals. He was taken aback at the sight of her, she was thin and pale. Maybe she was sick he thought. He was filled with dread, what if she has mental illness he wondered? What if all this had driven her insane? Oh, please God, not Mary.

Mary went about feeding her animals, she'd get over this she kept telling herself. Sometimes she sat and told the animals as she went around feeding them and watering them. Lilly was the only one who actually listened, and sometimes Jim. Jim had to because he was still a bit laid up and couldn't make it outside much.

When at last she finished she walked back inside and turned and locked the door. The hair on the back of her neck prickled as she slowly turned around. She gasped out loud, for there was Wally sitting at the table. She had let him get past her and into her house.

He had her rifle pointed at her. 'I just want to talk Mary, that's all. Sit yourself down girl and tell me what gives. Come on.'

Mary sat at the table 'oh piss off Wally you aren't going to use that.'

'And neither are you, Mary. And I'm not going anywhere till I find out what's wrong.' He put the gun on his knee. 'You could have killed Dan Mary.'

'If I wanted him dead, he'd be dead Wally, you know that. Next time I will not miss the bloody skunk, you make sure he knows that.'

'Alright Mary, do we assume here that you found out about the ring somehow?'

'Yes, and that somehow was Kathy. Now put the rifle down and clear off or I'll bloody shoot you with this one.' Mary brought the handgun out from under the table.

'You are not going to use that, Mary.'

A tear rolled down Mary's sunken cheek, she looked dreadful thought Wally.

'Please go Wally.' Her chin wiggled and the sight of it near broke Wally's heart.

He was desperate now and his voice was loud. 'But Mary he has looked everywhere, he's turned the place upside down. He is a man possessed.

Couldn't you just give him a break Mary? Just forgive him. He makes us all search for the damn thing Mary. All bloody day every bloody day.'

'What the hell are you talking about Wally? Sometimes I get more bloody sense from Lilly. Now I'll tell you again clear off and I hope they'll be bloody happy.'

'Who Mary? You hope who will be happy? For Christ's sake he lost it Mary. He'll get you another.'

'Lost what Wally? Lost what?'

Wally sighed, 'the ring Mary, he lost the damn ring and we have searched nonstop for it. Please Mary.'

Now Mary sighed and said flatly, 'tell him to search Kathy. Go on home now and tell him to ask Kathy where it is.'

Wally sucked in air; he'd got the gist of it. 'I'll be right back Mary; we can fix this.' And with that he ran all the way home Back at the camp Dan was sitting out on the log by himself. Wally sat beside him and trying to get his breath he gasped 'I know Dan. A mix up.... A mix up Dan. It's all a mix up....'

Dan stared at Wally, 'where have you been Wally?'

'Mary's....' He gasped for a bit longer and started to settle down. 'I know Dan. I know what's happened.'

Dan looked concerned 'have you been shot Wally? Wally?"

'No...... we talked. We got the drop on each other. Dan Mary told me to tell you Dan, she told me to tell you to search Kathy. For the ring.... she said Kathy knows where it is. Dan?'

Dan's mouth hung open and he squinted at Wally. It couldn't be, could it? Kathy had been acting strangely lately and Dan had thought she had a harmless school girly crush, but this?

'Well, is she home Dan?'

Dan got up and slowly walked inside. He went to Kathy, and she watched him approach. He said kindly, 'can you give me the ring Kathy, the one you stole from me?'

'No, it's mine' Kathy was yelling now and her mother came to her. 'What's this about Dan?'

'I think she has my ring, Mavis. Kathy how did Mary know you have it?'

'I was wearing it in town, I showed it to her. She didn't like it much, but she'll get over it. Won't she Dan? Won't she?'

'Oh Kathy' said Mavis and produced the ring from Kathy's bag. She handed it to Dan.

When Dan got to Mary's place, he found her laying on the floor next to Jim, sound asleep. It was clear on his way in that she had tended her animals and her garden every day.

Dan was astounded at the change in her, she was thin and pale with dark circles under her eyes. Her face was gaunt and her cheeks hollow. Jim made no move to go for him, but he crawled closer to the woman.

Tears found their way down Dan's cheeks as he sat there looking at her. He had left her, his Mary, he had left her to get like this.

He couldn't stop himself and he lowered his head and kissed her, 'waken sleeping beauty' he sobbed. 'Waken to me, but alas I am no prince.'

Mary stirred and, in her grogginess, she pushed him away and cried out. Dan lifted her into his arms and cuddled her, 'hush woman it is only me. I have come to beg your forgiveness my lady. And to beg you to hear me out.'

Mary struggled out of his arms and into a sitting position. Dan went on softly, 'I learned what happened from Wally. I am sorry Mary if I'd known I could have stood outside there and shouted to you. We have stopped searching for the ring I have it Mary. How could you believe I would get engaged to someone else? Tell me darling, how? Knowing how much I love you. I told you on the riverbank I could never love another.'

'Well Dan firstly you never gave it back to me, so I felt something had changed maybe irreparably. And then you came to see me only if you had a reason and that was not all that often. Kathy showed me my ring, which was no longer my ring Dan. Oh go away Dan I want to sleep.'

'Okay Mary, I am at fault. I woke up one night, can't remember which, and she was trying to lay beside me. I laughed and told her to go and get into bed and not be on my bed again. I should have addressed the problem then. Now everyone is upset.'

Mary picked up his hand and held it, 'give me some time Dan. It was wrong but it hurt. It hurt and I don't want to ever be that hurt again. See Dan, you can hurt me that much.'

'But I never would Mary.' Dan took her hand and gave her back the ring, 'I was looking for it Mary, I knew it was there somewhere. I couldn't look into your face knowing I had gone and lost it.'

Mary got up from the floor, 'can I have a cuddle Mary' he asked her?

She took him in her arms, and he cried, she cried. Dan lifted her into his arms and took her to bed. He lay with her the whole night and they both slept.

Mary woke just after sun up and turned around to look at an empty pillow. Her throat constricted; she must have dreamed it. Maybe she wanted him back so much she invented a reason for seeing the ring on Kathy's finger other than the one that was causing her such Pain.

Mary made her mind up in a flash, she'd go and confront the pair of them and anyone else in that damn long hut that wanted to side with them. She started pulling clean clothes on, muttering all the while to herself.

'He's my man damn it; she can bloody well find her own. Can't believe I let myself dream something like that. Oh, to hell with the pair of them.'

Mary threw herself across the bed and cried, her heartache was even worse than it ever was. Mary felt a hand on her shoulder, she didn't care who it was. When the hands had turned her over, she looked up into his beloved face. She sobbed a great sob and the two of them clung to each other until they were cried out.

Dan pushed her hair back from her face and smiled, 'what's all this fussing woman?' he pulled her gently in to his arms and went on, 'I told you that day on the banks of the great Murrumbidgee that I could never love another Mary.' He lifted her hand now and smiled softly, 'look my darling, you have your ring back. See?'

'Oh Dan' she cried.

'Where were you off to, all that throwing clothes on and muttering to your, self, woman.' He smiled tenderly as he held her arm up. 'This does look like yesterday's clothes and the day before that and the day before that.'

Mary looked down and grinned ruefully. 'Yes, I see, you're not so good yourself.'

They laughed together and Dan undressed her and made love to his woman.

After, they lay in each other's arms for hours and talked and loved. Dan experienced the joy that only loving her would bring.

'I'm sorry Dan.....'

'Nonsense woman, it was not your fault, none of it was. I want you to trust me more in future Mary. I am not the sort of man who goes around killing people and going off half cocked. I want you to know that I do despise myself for the things I've done but they hurt you Mary.'

Dan got off the bed and kneeling beside it he took Mary's hand. 'Will you marry me woman?'

Mary put her hand out and ruffled his hair, how she loved him. 'Yes Dan, I will. And never take this ring back again you might lose it.'

They both laughed and Dan kissed her tenderly. A shiver went through Mary, that thing which had awoken the first time he'd kissed her was awake again now. She pulled him into bed with her and undressed him.

———~w~◦◖◗◦◖◗◦◖◗◦◦~w~———

When Dan got home that afternoon it was to see an upset Mavis at the door.

Noreen was with her. 'What's going on girls' asked Dan tiredly?

Noreen stepped forward, 'they are leaving Dan, don't know where they think they will go.'

Dan looked at Mavis and said kindly 'what nonsense is this woman? We know each other better than this. Don't we? Tell me we do Mavis. It's just a misunderstanding and it's been cleared up. Come on put your things back and let's all work it out.'

'Thank you, Dan,' cried Mavis, 'but I'm sure Mary would like us to leave here and who can blame her. Kathy has done a wicked thing.'

Dan looked at the young girl who hadn't lifted her head. He spoke to Mavis, 'nay, she has done a childish thing. She has a school girl crush which she let get out of hand. Now Mary has her ring back and everything is fine.' He spoke gently to the girl now, 'you get over these things Kathy. Couple days from now you'll ask yourself what you ever saw in me. An old man not good looking, not very smart. One day a young man will come along, and he will have to stand before me and ask my blessing. Come on everybody back inside, we are family here.'

Dan took the tattered little suit case from Mavis, 'never in a million years would I let the two of you go on the road in such times as these, alone. If you were to go I would have to go with you and I don't want to.' At Mavis' bed he handed her the little case and held his arms out to her. Mavis and Kathy cried in his arms. 'Now come on the two of you get busy moving back in.'

He turned to Noreen who had tears in her eyes, 'and why have you got the miseries' he asked? 'I have invited Mary for dinner is that okay?' Dan felt the tension dissipate and he went and turned the radio on. 'What are you grinning about' he asked Ben?

Chapter 13

*I*t was mid-March when they got a light rain and Dan and Mary decided to start seeding. They worked from sunup until dark hardly stopping to eat or drink.

Mostly Dan had a drink or something to eat as he drove the tractor and stopped only when Mary had lunch with him. He taught Mary how and she took her turn at the wheel.

Anyone who was at home came out to watch, as the tractor went round and round. There were some broken hearts for Lilly, and someone always sat with her. It wasn't just the horse but to them it was the end of an era and they all felt it.

Mary had also mastered the truck but still rode Lilly in to town to get the mail and such. Mary could drive the truck if she had to but didn't like to whereas she loved to ride Lilly. Dan was talking about getting a smaller car for the women to use, the truck wasn't very suitable. Mary only ever saw herself harnessing the cart to the horse for the trip into town.

In three weeks, they had done the eighty acres in wheat. The week before that they had put a half-acre of vegies in. They had depleted a lot of their stores in the cellar, it was about half full and the women had started to ration though not terribly strict. They were still getting meat and they had money to buy food if they had to. They would put a half-acre of food in each fortnight for the market to for a month then go back to every month.

Dan took Mary home in the truck and as she was getting out, he said, 'Mary I want to come in and talk to you about something. Okay?'

'Of course, Dan.'

Mary got Dan a coffee and sat at the table with him. Dan played with his cup in silence for a minute and then looked up at Mary. 'Mary, I want to get married. Soon.'

'I know Dan, so do I. I can't wait Dan.'

'We have a problem Mary, see I want to live with you....'

Mary stared at him puzzled. 'Of course. You want to live here? Oh, Dan I think I know. How are you going to leave your family over there?'

'What do we do Mary? And then there's the boys and school. It's a headache Mary. I've tried and tried but I don't know what to do.' He reached across and took her hand in his. 'I love it here Mary but I think the long hut needs me there for a bit longer. Mary, are you willing to come and live with me?'

'Yes Dan. But I want to bring my bed. It's huge and it's comfortable.'

'No argument there. Mary maybe we could get busy and build a couple of rooms on to the long hut. Some of the others are.'

'That's a wonderful idea darling. We can come here sometimes to do maintenance and upkeep, maybe weekends with the boys. Yes, let's do it Dan, make a couple of rooms.'

'Will you move in soon baby' Dan stood up and came round the table? He pulled her up into his arms, the relief was euphoric. He had expected her to oppose the idea.

'How soon Dan?"

'Tomorrow. Oh, bugger it all I can't do this. I'm not sleeping I can't keep my mind on anything but you. I worry about you here by yourself. Come on Mary, please.'

'But Dan, what will people say?'

'To hell with them Mary. Come on baby we've got a bit of time on our hands. We could start building our rooms day after tomorrow. If we are living together, we could wait a bit longer to get married and have more money to spend on your wedding day Mary.'

'Dan! That was emotional blackmail.' She threw her arms around him and kissed him. Dan held her to him; he had dared to dream, and this was it.

Dan and Mary accompanied by Wally had made several trips to the dump and cut down four trees. Now Ben was helping them build their two rooms. Mary had moved her bed in a week ago and everyone was glad she was there. She took the kids to school in the cart and sometimes Noreen. Noreen had taken on two days a week at the hospital and most of that was in the day time. Mary took Lilly to pick her up along with the others on the cart. Everyone enjoyed these leisurely trips to and from town on the cart. It was just the thing after a long hard day. One or two of the others always accompanied her to.

Some of the other residents of the long hut had made separate rooms and it was freeing up living space in the long hut. One night early in April when Dan and Mary's place was nearly done, they were all sitting around after tea. 'Who thinks they will leave one day' Dan asked?

There were no takers. 'Are you all so happy here' Dan asked again?

The answer came from Samuel, 'yes, I am, I love this place. I hope nobody ever leaves, it would break my poor old heart.' He laughed and everyone laughed with him.

'I want to stay forever to' said Ben, 'but I don't think I will ever move out of the big room here.'

'Well, there is no need for anyone to move out unless you want to. It is warm in here,' said Dan. Two families one of five and one of four had moved out into separate dwellings. Noreen and her family were in the process of moving out after making two rooms onto the side of the long hut.

Noreen said now 'I just love that we eat together and spend our time together. We only really intend to sleep out there.'

Dan and Mary had taken the last available space on the back wall of the long hut. This wall would afford them some warmth in winter. The young men had built a shelter on the end of the hut but only Wally and Ron slept out there now.

They moved into the rooms four weeks after they started the build. Dan had given his bed to Ben who had been sleeping on the floor. Mary and Dan were happy at last. 'I am living with the woman

I love' Dan replied to Mary's enquiry concerning the grin that never left his face.

The only person not happy with Dan and Mary's arrangement was Bryce, the boy was distraught and refused to have anything to do with his father. He'd been that way since Mary moved into the long hut with them. Mary tried to talk to him, but he refused to listen. He started going to bed early and getting up late.

One day Dan took the boy outside on the log with him. 'Bryce you can't go on like this son, you are not eating and you mope from the time you get up to the time you get back into bed.'

Bryce pulled his arm away from his father's grip and sneered. 'Well, I'm fuckin sorry you don't like it.'

Bryce found himself laying over his father's knee having his backside smacked. Dan pulled him up in his lap and put his arms around the boy who was so like him. 'Bryce, stop this, Mary loves you....'

'She loves you. I don't I hate you.'

'Bryce, Mary is capable of loving lots of people you know.'

'Fine let her get on with it.'

'I know you love her Bryce but ....'

'I would have married her, unlike you, you mongrel. You don't bloody deserve her.'

Dan searched his sons face and his own mind for a solution to their problem.

This was serious and he hated to see the kid suffer like this. 'Please Bryce, I love you.....'

'Yeah, I see. Well Dad I'm out of here. You have belted my arse for the last time. I hate you.'

Bryce turned and walked away; he spoke to no one for the rest of that day. Dan worried, when he spoke to Mary she offered to go back home. 'No, I don't want that, Mary. I don't. That's not gunna happen Mary.' He held her to him gently, 'I won't let anything come between us again Mary, it nearly broke me and you to.'

He went into Bryce's room later that night to say goodnight to the boy who had retired earlier. Mary heard the yell in the next room in fact they heard it in the long hut. 'Bryce! Bryce!' Dan ran back into his and Mary's room followed by a sleepy Kane.

Mary grabbed Dan and held him 'what is it, Dan?'

'He's gone Mary, he's taken his clothes his coat and his blanket.'

Dan ran to the long house and breathed a sigh of relief for there was Bryce asleep on the floor where their beds had been. He sat beside him and picked his son up into his arms. Bryce woke up and tried to struggle, 'I'm not coming out there Dad.'

'Alright son, it's alright. If this is what you need to do, then so be it.'

'Are you crying dad?' Bryce lifted his hand and wiped away the tears on Dans cheeks. He sat up and looked into his father's face, 'I thought you didn't love me.'

'Well, I bloody do Bryce, I love you with all my heart.'

'Mum used to say that.'

'I know.'

Mary had arrived in the long house and seeing the two of them decided to give them some space and she sat with Kane at the table. Kane sat close to her and she put her arm around him.

Dan stroked the boys hair and said softly, 'I'll bring your bed in Bryce if you want to stay here for a bit longer. I know how you feel son, I know how much I love Mary. If I lost her, I'd never get over it. And who knows one day in the future she might decide I am too old and leave me.'

Bryce studied his father's face now and his face changed. 'Dad I'm sorry, but I do want to stay in here for a bit. I loved it in here dad. This was my first home and mum...... You know.'

'I know son I know, but don't hate me son. Please, never hate me.' Dan sobbed as the boy cuddled into him. 'I didn't mean it dad.'

'Well okay. You wanna help me bring your bed back in here son?'

That night as Mary, Kane and Dan went to leave the long hut and Bryce, they said goodnight to him. Bryce walked up to Mary and said, 'can you forgive me Mary?'

Mary looked down and saw Dan, the boy was the image of his father and her heart broke. She fell on her knees and put her arms around him. When his arms went around her it did indeed feel like Dan. 'I love you Mary' he whispered. She smiled and he kissed her lips. Mary couldn't have moved if her life depended on it. The boy stepped back and got into bed. Dan had tears in his eyes and so did Kane and Mary. Ben and almost everyone else had tears in their eyes. It felt to them like the boy had come home. It was Ben who said 'don't worry, we'll see he's alright.'

———

Life returned to normal for Dan and Mary and the boys except that Bryce still slept in the long hut. Dan knew it had as much to do with his mother as anything. The day after the boy had ran back to the long hut Dan had taken him to visit his mother's grave. He'd got down and held the little boy as he cried, the sobs wracking his little body. Dan held him, he knew this was the cry he needed to have.

When the sobbing had subsided and Dan stood up, he looked up at Dan. His little tear-stained face so full of sadness it broke the big man's heart. 'Dad, I'm sorry. I will settle for second best in Mary's heart because it is you who are first. But dad, marry her.'

'I will son, soon. You could be my best man, Bryce. What do you say?'

'Yeah, dad me and Kane hay?' Bryce turned and kissed the cross on his mother's grave and turned around and held Dan's hand all the way home, held it tightly.

Chapter 14

*D*an stood at the door of the long hut and marvelled yet again at the feeling he got when he looked upon the green fields. The wheat was up a few inches, and everything looked green. He decided he loved this time of year.

It was July 15th, and He was marrying the love of his life the next day, Saturday the 16th of July in 1938. Mary had gone home to her shanty, telling Dan it was bad luck for the bride and groom to see each other tomorrow. So Wally and Ben had put a few bob together to take Dan out on the town.

Dan had protested, 'I can't drink and drive Mary's truck' he'd said. 'Not as long as she has that bloody riding crop. Don't forget I've felt what that mongrel of a thing can do.'

'You Dan' the two men said? Ben was trying not to laugh and Wally stared wide eyed. He wasn't sure if he wanted to know.

'Oh, just bloody forget it.'

'Well Wally can drive.'

So, the three men accompanied by every other man in the long hut went off into town. Wally had to be carried out and put in the back. Wally had to be on deck the next day to go as Dans witness.

It was to be an informal ceremony officiated by the priest who had done the honours at Iris and the babies funeral. Dan found that he liked the man.

Dan was dressed in his very best along with everyone else. He was having trouble with his stomach, he hadn't drank for so long. Kane had gone to Mary's as he was going to give her away and Bryce had elected to stay with his father. Dan had smiled down at him and said gently 'thanks buddy.'

Dan stood at the small altar, his stomach was churning, he couldn't believe it. In a few hours he'd be married to Mary and all of his dreams come true. How he loved her.

Dan heard a murmur at the back of him and his heart quickened. He turned expecting to see Mary and Kane. But instead, he looked into the smiling face of Jack.

Dan took the few steps to him and threw his arms around him. 'Jesus Jack, it's bloody good to see you, old mate.' Tears trickled from the big man's eyes and Jack sniffed.

Then Dan was aware of a tall heavy-set man behind him and he let Jack go to shake hands with the mayor. 'Good of you to come' he said, 'Mary will be happy about that.'

'It's my pleasure, and if I can wangle an invite I would like to come to the reception. Where is it?"

'Yes, well we are celebrating at the long... at the community hut.'

Dan hadn't expected it, but the mayor's face lit up and he beamed a smile at Dan. 'Excellent Dan, I missed the funeral, I was in hospital down in Melbourne.'

A lady came in and sat at the organ and the mayor and Jack sat down. Dan cast his eyes around at the people he loved, the family he loved. He stood waiting for Mary, he knew his hands had started shaking.

He watched the doors as Mary came through them. He got a grin on his face and tears in his eyes. As she came towards him, he laughed and cried in equal measure. His throat was dry and he realised he'd stopped breathing. He gulped air into his lungs as she took the last few steps to him.

She slipped her arm through his and smiled up at him tears in her eyes. Kane stood behind her and when the priest said who gives this woman to be married, Kane was having trouble with the words. To his horror he whined 'I do'.

They were married and Dan kissed his bride and put all his love into it. He needed no top up and he also knew that where ever Iris was she was happy for him. A tear slid down his face when he thought of the sacrifice, she'd made so he could be so happy.

Back at the long hut the tables were laden as well as they had been for Iris' funeral. Once again, the people he loved had done him proud. Mary was beautiful and she had worn a dress for the occasion. Dan thought he would love her in anything but he now found he preferred her in strides.

Jack was on his best behaviour and seemed for the most part to be happy for the couple. Dan sidled up to him now and asked how he had been.

'Yeah, I'm alright Dan. I hope you don't mind me being here mate, Ben wrote to me. He reminded me about my behaviour last time I came and gave me a most dire warning Dan.'

They both laughed and Dan said 'it's good to see you mate. And I see you are now a lieutenant.' Dan shook his hand and smiled, 'well done young man I always thought you'd make us proud.' Dan walked away from the people a little and said quietly, 'that other business Jack?"

Jack smiled and said quietly 'it was just as you said Dan. When I got back to Melbourne, I told her that my father had put me wise to her and the kid aint mine.' The two men laughed softly; Dan heart swelled. Jack went on, 'well she told me, "no and thank God for that." I never saw her again. Glad you and Mary are happy you deserve it. I heard about young Mathew.'

'Who from' asked Dan curious?

'Mathew.'

'How is that?"

'Oh, sorry you probably don't know, he's down there with me now, he joined up. He tells a story which I doubt to be the right one. Then he told me you'd turfed him out and I knew he must have done something. I don't see him much and I'm glad of that, I never liked him.'

The two men talked for a little while and then went to join in the fun. And they all had fun, even the mayor had fun. There were some townspeople there and Josh was amongst them. Dan looked across at him, he was talking to Kathy and Dan saw the spark between them. Thank God he thought to himself. Yes, everything was working out at long last.

Later that evening he found himself alone with his new bride. Dan and Mary would spend a few days by themselves at Mary's shanty. As Dan lay back in her arms, he felt a contentment and a peace that he never thought would be his. And it was largely because Mary was his. Bryce had gotten over his jealousy but had not yet moved into his bedroom with Dan and Mary.

He'd been surprised to see Jack at the wedding he said this to Mary now. She smiled at him and said softly, 'he seems to have gotten himself sorted Dan. I'm glad.'

'Did you see Kathy chatting away to Josh?'

'Yes, I did Dan. They looked to me as though they were getting very chummy.' Dan laughed softly and turned and looked at Mary, 'may I kiss the bride, Mary?

Just this once like?'

Life had gotten back to some semblance of normality since the wedding a month ago. Dan was at his favourite past time now, watching the grass grow. Mary came up behind him and slipped her arm around him. He smiled at her and kissed her, 'did I tell you how very beautiful you are Mary?'

'Not today my love.'

He looked thoughtful now, 'and what do you make of the crop this year Mary? Do you think it's as good as last years?'

'Yes, I do Dan. Just about three months now and we'll see how good it is. You are quite a farmer you know Dan. We've got market next week to. You are quite a hit there to. You love it don't you darling?'

Dan smiled lazily at her 'yep, nearly as much as I love you. Do you think Bryce will move in with us Mary?"

Mary nodded 'he needs this time with his mum.'

Dan nodded, 'I have asked a lot of them and you and all the people here, haven't I? In my hurry to be married to you.' He turned and taking her in his arms he hugged her. He sighed contentedly.

It was early in November when Dan and Mary and Samuel

decided it was time to harvest. They got a bumper crop again and Dan and Mary made nine hundred pounds each. They spent a few hundred on their two rooms and made improvements to the long hut.

Christmas of '38 was even bigger and better than the last. Jack came home for one thing and brought home his intended. He contributed to the kids' toys and the food.

This year it was Jack who asked Dan for his blessing and when the time came if he would be permitted to build two rooms for him and his family. The vote was unanimous, and Dan breathed easy. Though he knew war was coming and he feared for Jack and Wally and all the others. Dan feared for himself.

In February of 1939 Mary found she was expecting and Dan lay and cried in her arms. He cried for the little girl they'd lost and everyone else. But he was happy. Mary told him she thought it was a boy, but Dan was adamant she was having a girl. And in August of that year, they found he was right.

'Hello Liberty Rose' he said as he held the tiny girl in his arms. He smiled softly at Mary, 'thank you my love, she is nearly as beautiful as you.'

Chapter 15

ife had been pretty settled for the people of the long hut for some time. One day as they stood at the side of the long hut Dan, and Noreen and some of the others stood watching as a car pulled up on the other side of the garden. Two men got out and set up some equipment that didn't look at all familiar to them.

'What do you reckon it is' asked Noreen worry lines appearing on her face?

Dan shrugged, 'where's Mary' he asked and sang out to her? He turned and saw her at the door to the kitchen. She turned and went back inside. Dan looked at her and knew she was up to something, though what? He and the others followed her.

Dan spoke 'what is this, Mary? Are they surveyors out there?'

Mary looked up at the frightened faces and smiled. 'They are Dan,' she said. 'They are going to measure off four acres and these four acres will be signed over to you all. It is time you owned this home of yours.'

Dan stared at this woman he loved; he was speechless. He wasn't sure how it would be worked out, but he fell on his knees before her. 'Are you sure Mary? Can this be so?'

And so it was that in September of 1939 the long hut became a co-op and was signed over to the residents who became the legal owners. It was decided that Dan would be a part of it. The people wanted him to be part of it.

They had bought a Ford Ute; they were independent at last, and they could get all the kids in the back. Some of the residents now planned more rooms and eventually the long hut would be a kitchen living space and a bedroom at one end for the single men.

Each month Mary and Dan went to the market, and they now averaged a whopping twelve pound each. Nearly every family in the community had at least one-member working. Still, everyone put in the kitty for everyday expenses and kept a small portion for themselves.

It was farther decided that the monies at the end of the year from the crops would be split into thirds. One for Mary, one for Dan and one for the community. Mary had put all the money back in her nest egg she had taken for the truck and tractor now with help from Dan.

It was unbelievable to everyone that every year the community would have a share of five to six hundred pounds. Some of the blokes who had the time asked Dan if they would be able to help him. Dan smiled and told them it would be greatly appreciated.

Mary still insisted that she buy lambs to eat up the leftover hay from the paddocks. These lambs went for a high price in town at the market once they had been butchered and salted or smoked.

The price of wheat went up markedly in the summer of '39 because of the dustbowl effect. The dust bowl didn't hamper them unduly because they hadn't farmed the land much before and they seemed to get just enough rain. The price of their goods at the market did not go up either because Dan and the others could see that other people were going hungry now.

War broke out in September of that year and their young men started shipping out for parts unknown. Mary coming in the back door one day was brought to a halt. Dan had a letter and a shocked look on his face. 'They want me to join up Mary.' He looked at her sadly, 'it's a request at this stage. Oh Mary I can't bear to leave you.'

'That's nonsense Dan, you are a primary producer, you are needed here. Well, somebody has got to feed the army.'

'But Mary… is a few acres enough?'

'Probably Dan but don't forget you own this place to. You know, jointly with me Dan.'

She laughed as he looked bewildered. 'This place Mary?'

Laughing, Mary sat on his knee and slipped her arm around his neck. 'You signed a second paper Dan, that was to put your name on the deeds here. It's a good job you got your looks mister. Now you own more land than I do.'

Dan stared at her open mouthed for some seconds. 'Sometimes woman you amaze me. Could it be that you have saved my bacon yet again?' He looked down at the papers, 'they'll take Wally and Ron and probably Dennis. Jesus Mary I am afraid, for everyone.'

'I know Dan. Do you think …. It'll be a long time?'

'Yes Mary, they are saying it won't last long, but I've got a bad feeling. You know Mary, with such great countries involved it'll be a hell of a fight. And this one will go down to the wire and then some I think.'

Dan took Mary and they went off to army HQ in Melbourne. Indeed, they told Dan they needed him here to grow as much damn wheat as he could. The sharp-eyed sergeant laughed and said, 'I suspect you have flat feet anyway so stay at home son.'

Dan took Mary to see the sights of Melbourne. Mary loved it and said to Dan 'maybe we should come and live here Dan.'

Dan bestowed a look of derision on her before he smiled, 'Never say those words to me again woman. I would hate to have to bring the boys back here and I never will bring Libby here.' Dan smiled 'I'd like to try and see Jack though Mary.'

Dan and Mary stayed at the Grand Hotel in Melbourne for one night. When the taxi pulled up Mary stood on the kerb looking up. She was dressed in a skirt and blouse, but she felt shabby. 'Dan, this place must cost a fortune.'

'Near enough me darlin but we can think of it as our honeymoon. He picked up the suitcase and walked on saying 'nothings too good for my girl you know that honey.' He smiled at her as she slipped her hand through his arm and hung on.

It was a night neither of them would forget. Mary could not believe that people lived like this. At the dinner table that night Mary said, 'Dan these women are so beautiful.'

'None of them can hold a candle to you Mary, you are just right,

I told you that.

And you don't need to pile on the make-up. If you're finished sweetheart, I'd like to get up to bed.'

———⁓⦿⦾⦿⦾⁓———

It was a dark day when Dan learned they had sent Jack overseas. It was darker still when Wally got called up the following year. Dan's heart was in tatters when Kathy signed up and went into the air force. She would be a part of traffic control and was set on getting her pilots licence to test fly planes. After that Josh was a regular visitor at the place.

It was in August of '44 when they got word that Jack was missing presumed dead. He had lost his life they thought, while taking part along with his unit in the fighting along the Kokoda track.

Wally was wounded in '43 and got sent home. Dan went to Melbourne to bring him home and listened to Wally's despair. He had been shot in the left arm and it had been rendered pretty useless. He couldn't straighten it.

'Jesus Dan I'll never get my job on the railways back.'

Dan hadn't been able to help himself and had thrown his arm around Wally's shoulder. Now gently rubbing his back he said 'well we need to feed these peoples Wally. There is too much to be done here to keep this country going to drop your bundle lad and as for your contribution to the war, you gave your arm.' Dan smiled at him now, 'with you home to help me we can have an acre of vegies in all the time to take to market. We can hunt pigs and rabbits and anything else people can eat. Hunger Wally, that's the enemy here and it is insidious. And I am afraid of it Wally.'

Wally nodded his head, 'I remember Dan. Remember how it twists your stomach until it hurts. All night long mate, wasn't so bad in the daytime but the nights.'

Dan sat beside Wally in the train looking thoughtful then 'there is a small piece of land which is right in the bend of the river, probably about half an acre, maybe a bit more. I might collar that and use it. We can do something with that. Maybe a milking cow or something.

Or we could keep the lambs a bit longer until they are full grown and get a few more pounds off them. But I will need help Wally we'll need to fence it off. With you we can do it.'

Dan was rewarded with one of Wally's beautiful, big grins.

———〜〜〰〜〜〜———

Life went on with Wally's return though Dan knew he'd never get over Jack's death. He kept himself busy and his efforts to feed the people of the community and the town were tireless. It was August of '44 and the war was in it's let's slog it out phase.

Dan was in the paddock one day by the river fixing the fence around the acre in the bend. He'd decided to put ten ewes on it and every year they'd have about ten lambs for slaughter. The skins were also sold to a tannery in Melbourne.

A vehicle pulled up and a man in uniform got out. Dan could see he was an officer but couldn't quite make him out. He wore his cap down over his face. When he neared Dan, he lifted his head and pushed his cap back.

Dan's heart skipped a beat when he recognised the man. Unhappily he rose to his feet and walked to meet Mathew. 'What do you want here' he asked curtly?

Mathew held out his hand and Dan shook it briefly. Mathew smiled sadly now, 'I have come to thank you for the beating you gave me. I have never forgotten it. You see Dan, I never cared about anything before that, not even myself.

Before I tagged along with you my family were attacked. I was thirteen and four men attacked them and left my family dead.'

Dan sucked in air, 'I heard about that. Down near Deniliquin, wasn't it? Shit Mathew why did you never say?'

Mathew shrugged his shoulders and looked down; he kept his eyes down as he said in a tiny voice. 'That night I saw what happened to Mary I nearly died. It took me ages to get over that to. Though I never really got over any of it.' He looked up at the fence Dan had been working on and Dan could see that pain had distorted his face. 'I just wanted to come and ask you to forgive me and think of me a little more kindly like. I am not looking to be bosom buddies just nod to me if you see me around. Though I doubt I will ever come back here. Too many memories here now. Would you tell Mary I am sorry Dan?'

'I don't know what to say Mathew, except I am very sorry. Jesus Mathew.'

'It's okay Dan, I am not here for anything else other than to make amends. I never said anything about what I saw that night because Mary didn't.' A sheepish smile made its way across Mathews face and he blushed 'I was in love with her and I would have kept her secret forever Dan. You couldn't have dragged that out of me even with your crop Dan.' He Laughed softly and looked about, 'I miss this place I still think of it as home.' He swung around and looked at Dan now. 'I wish to God I had killed those blokes Dan, but I saw my mother and sister there and I had to run away. Like a dog I ran and ran.'

A great sob escaped Mathew now and Dan put his arms around the man and held him as he cried.

When he'd finished Dan stepped back and looked at him, 'I'll see that the others know Mathew. Come home whenever you want mate.'

Mathew smiled and then 'I heard what happened to Jack, I'm sorry Dan.' He looked down 'and Wally and as far as I know Ron is still in a New Guinea hospital.'

'Why' asked Dan?

'I'm sorry Dan thought you'd know by now. He got malaria and may be sent home.'

'Shit! And you Mathew, are you going to have to go' Dan asked softly now?

'Oh, I've been Dan, went across with Jacks mob.' He gave a laugh 'I got a bullet in the arse but I look like going back over soon. Probably get malaria with Ron.' He looked at Dan, 'that belting you gave me made me realise that if I wanted to be treated right, I had to act right. I'd been nothing but sorry for myself and it was a horrendous thing to do. To just run off. I'm sorry for what I did to Sarah to, I liked her.'

Dan nodded 'me and Mary got married.'

'I know Jack told me. Congratulations Dan and on your little girl as well.'

Mathew held his hand out to Dan now 'well goodbye Dan, I gotta get back to Melbourne. I'm glad I came; it's been a heavy weight to carry but I'm a man now. I hope. Will you tell her Dan, tell Mary I'm sorry, so sorry?'

Dan smiled and told him he would. 'I'm sorry to Mathew, maybe if I'd known....'

'Yeah, I know Dan, but we are alright now. The horrors of war have a way of making this all seem like.... well. How's Wally Dan?'

'He's going alright Mathew; I keep him pretty busy. We have stepped up our efforts to produce good food. We remember Mathew, what it's like to be starving don't we?'

Mathew smiled, 'I also heard that Mary had made some acres over to you legally Dan. Not many like her about.'

'Yeah, well we made the acres a sort of co-op so every one of us owns them.'

'Well goodbye Dan, can I call in to see you when I'm going through. I will never again cause you any trouble, you have my word on that.'

'Anytime Mathew.' Dan took the man in his arms and hugged him and Mathew hugged him back. 'I'm glad you called in Mathew. Drop us a line sometimes, when you can and let us know you're okay.'

'Thanks Dan, I will.'

The war ended in September of '45 and Ron arrived home in November. The people of the community were planning a big Christmas. They had Wally and Ron back and Kathy was coming home on leave for it. It had been agreed that they would write to Mathew care of the army and ask him if he would be coming home for Christmas. He had replied that he would if possible and thanked them.

Ron had applied to get his job back on the railways but had had to take a job as fireman on a train there. It was the local train which ran wheat to the silos two or three days a week. One of the old men in the gang was retiring soon so Ron was promised his job.

The people were sad because Maynard had been taken to hospital and wasn't likely to come home. He'd had pneumonia and was medicated so he knew very little. Maynard died before the end of November. The doctors said his heart had failed in the end.

Libby now went to school with the boys, they adored her. Dan had gotten to work and built a small room for her. Then he had gotten to work lining the rooms and had painted them. In fact, the whole place had been done up. The people loved their home and especially now that it belonged to them. It gave them a feeling of permanence and an extra sense of security.

The kids had all done well at school and Kane and three of the others had made it in to high school. Dan decided to give them something extra for their efforts he was so proud of them. He'd bought them each a fountain pen in a nice box.

They had had bumper crops each year and had a tidy little nest egg as well as each family having savings of their own. Wally had bought himself a Ute and did odd jobs round about. Dan had put him in charge of the ewes and ram and all their progeny. He got a percentage of the money that brought in. Wally was happy and Dan breathed a sigh of relief.

On Christmas eve Dan sat out the front on the logs which still served as an outdoor setting. He was thinking of Jack and whether or not he had suffered at the end. He wished there was some way they could know. He lifted his cup up and threw his head back to swallow the last mouthful. He choked on it. He'd seen a ghost, or an apparition.

Jack smiled down at him, 'g'day Dan, how's it going old man?'

Dan sat looking up trying to get his breath. Jack sat down beside him and pounded him on the back. Dan got his breath and sat looking at the man he'd just been grieving.

'Jack, it can't be....'

Jack laughed and carried on rubbing Dan's back. 'You alight there now Dan?'

'Jack Jack you're so skinny. Don't tell me.... Oh no Jack' Dan was shaking his head from side to side. 'We heard you were gone Jack.'

'Yep, the japs got me Dan. I was shot, I took one in the shoulder and one to the side of my head. I lay in the jungle I dunno how long. Anyhow some fuzzy wuzzyies that didn't speak a word of English got me to a mission hospital. No body at the hospital spoke any English either but they took care of me. I don't even know how long I was there I couldn't remember if I was Arthur or Martha. Well anyway I finally clicked who I was and I got out of bed and went back to fight. I met up with some chaps from another unit and well anyway on the way back to the front we encountered the Japanese so we off into the jungle again. Soon after that I joined up with a unit of Americans and fought with them for a while. Eventually we were taken prisoner, about three months later I think. I didn't even know I'd been reported missing. Anyway Dan, here I am.'

Dan threw his arms around Jack, 'thank God Jack, thank God.' Dan studied Jack's thin face and hollowed cheeks. 'You had to go through it again Jack only worse. I have heard how you blokes got treated.'

Jack lowered his head 'I'm hopeful Dan that I will get past this and forget it in time, though I do not hold my breath. In the end it was a unit of Aussie commandos, the second eight, who came for us.' He took a deep breath now and went on, 'how are Wally and Ron?'

'Yeah, they are okay mate.'

'Mathew caught up with me in New Guinea, but we'd only just met up when he got it Dan.'

'Got it?'

'Yeah, I was talking to him and then he just got it in the back and died in my arms.'

Dan looked down 'he came to see me Jack, all was forgiven. Thank goodness. We had invited him home for Christmas and he had accepted. Jack last time we met you had an intended. I don't wish to appear nosey mate but....'

'Yeah I had an intended Dan. I went to see her when I got back but she wasn't home. Anyhow her mother answered the door and told me they'd thought I was dead. She also told me that my intended had met another bloke and was now engaged to him.' Jack smiled grimly at Dan, 'you win some you lose some I guess mate. So here I am Dan.'

'Yes Jack, here you are and thank God for it. I'm sorry to hear this Jack, I don't know what to say.

'Not much you can say mate, I'll get over it. Jesus it's good to be home Dan. I have dreamed and wished for this many times. Night after night for so long. So long Dan, that I never thought I'd make it.' There was a sob in Jacks voice as he said, 'I had given up Dan.'

Dan sat looking into Jacks poor face, how he had changed. He looked older than himself. Dan suddenly knew a deep sadness that hurt. He knew that it would take Jack a long time to get back into some semblance of his former self. He also knew that he would be there to help him every step of the way.

'Heard you got a baby girl Dan any chance I could meet her?'

'Sure thing Jack.'

When Jack walked into the long hut where everyone was getting ready to sit down for tea it was bedlam. Everyone gathered around and Jack looked across at a little girl standing back. 'Mary' he breathed. Dan smiled.

Mary came over and brought her little girl. 'This is Libby Jack; she is almost six.'

Jack shook her hand and smiled, 'The image of her mother I see. That's a good thing Dan.'

Everyone laughed and Jack was back in the bosom of his family. He cried and Dan held him. 'It'll get better Jack. There is too much work to be done to cry for long. The country is in a bad way. We are here Jack, we are here. I'll help you all I can.'

Ron and Dennis shook his hand, hugged him, and told him welcome home. Jack looked around and found Wally. noting the crooked arm he smiled knowingly and said 'nice to see you again Wally.'

Wally shook hands with him, 'good to have you back man. We'll get the meat back on your bones mate and the laughter back in your craw.'

Jack wiped his eyes and smiled at Wally 'thanks mate, it's bloody lovely to be back here. I've lay awake dreaming of this moment for so long. The old place looks good, it's a credit to you all.' He smiled. 'I believe you own it now Dan.'

'Yes mate we own it. You are with us Jack.'

Suddenly Jack looked at Dan, 'my God man, is this Kane? Jesus he's nearly as tall as me. And Bryce' Jack went on getting reacquainted with the kids and then the adults. It was good to be home. It was the homecoming he'd wished for but never thought would be his. He wouldn't stuff it up again he promised himself.

Dan turned to Mary and taking her in his arms he smiled softly, 'merry Christmas Mrs Roberts.'

Mary smiled back at him, 'same to you my darling. And Santa clause has delivered us a brand-new baby due in June.'

'Oh Mary, just when I thought I had it all. You have done it again woman. Let's go back to the shanty tonight baby. Home Mary, home.'

Mary took Dan's face in her hands and kissed him tenderly, 'It's a boy this time my love.'

Dan grinned and nodded, 'you might be right woman. That's okay Mary, I have my Libby. She is the apple of my eye. I love you Mary, I thank God for you every single day. Remember that day we kissed down by the river Mary? And you held my hand. I loved you more that day than I had ever thought you could love someone.'

A hush fell over the place and Dan and Mary watched as Kathy and Joshua stood up and moved together to the middle of the floor. Dan put his hand up for silence, he knew in his heart there was even more good news. Yes, this was a Christmas to match any damn Christmas. Dan's heart sang so that you could possibly hear it in heaven.

THE END